Libertarians, Socialists, and Other Third Parties

Bridey Heing and
Erica Grove, Book Editors

GREENHAVEN
PUBLISHING

Published in 2022 by Greenhaven Publishing, LLC
29 East 21st Street, New York, NY 10010

Articles in Greenhaven Publishing anthologies are often edited for length to meet page
requirements. In addition, original titles of these works are changed to clearly present
the main thesis and to explicitly indicate the author's opinion. Every effort is made to
ensure that Greenhaven Publishing accurately reflects the original intent of the authors.
Every effort has been made to trace the owners of the copyrighted material.

Cover image: Ink Drop/Shutterstock.com.

Library of Congress Cataloging-in-Publication Data

Names: Heing, Bridey, editor. | Grove, Erica M., editor.
Title: Libertarians, socialists, and other third parties / Bridey Heing and
    Erica Grove, book editors.
Description: First edition. | New York : Greenhaven Publishing, 2022. |
    Series: Current controversies | Includes bibliographical references and
    index. | Audience: Ages 15+ | Audience: Grades 10–12 | Summary: "This volume
    examines the role of third parties in American politics and the extent
    to which they can exercise influence"— Provided by publisher.
Identifiers: LCCN 2020050226 | ISBN 9781534507906 (library binding) | ISBN
    9781534507883 (paperback) | ISBN 9781534507913 (ebook)
Subjects: LCSH: Third parties (United States politics)—Juvenile
    literature. | Political culture—United States—Juvenile literature.
Classification: LCC JK2261 .L53 2022 | DDC 324.273—dc23
LC record available at https://lccn.loc.gov/2020050226

Manufactured in the United States of America

Website: http://greenhavenpublishing.com

Chapter 3: Can Third Parties Represent American Values?

Yes: Third Parties Are Just as Capable of Representing American Values as the Two Major Parties

Jim Jonas

The two major political parties have formed an electoral system that makes it nearly impossible for third-party candidates to have a fair shot. Increased competition in the form of third-party candidates would make for a healthier electoral system and encourage candidates to better represent the average American's values.

Oishimaya Sen Nag

Historically, some third-party and independent candidates have won a significant number of votes from the Electoral College and in the popular vote. This viewpoint examines ten cases in which third-party candidates were able to gain support in presidential elections and make a difference in the political system.

Lauren Gambino

The Democratic Socialists of America (DSA) has gained traction in recent years, particularly among young voters. This is likely because young people are increasingly disillusioned by capitalism since they came of age during the global financial crisis of 2007–2008.

Gene H. Bell-Villada

Writer and political philosopher Ayn Rand's libertarian ideals of limited government, spending cuts, and the protection of individual liberties have resonated with mainstream Republicans in recent years.

No: Ultimately, Third Parties Cannot Sufficiently Represent the Values of Average Americans

Marshall Terrill

Adding a third party into the mix likely would not solve the problem of political polarization. In fact, countries that have more than two major political parties are often polarized as well.

Chapter 4: Do Third Parties Have a Future in the United States?

Yes: Third-Party Candidates Could Play a Bigger Role in the Future of US Politics

Foreword

"Controversy" is a word that has an undeniably unpleasant connotation. It carries a definite negative charge. Controversy can spoil family gatherings, spread a chill around classroom and campus discussion, inflame public discourse, open raw civic wounds, and lead to the ouster of public officials. We often feel that controversy is almost akin to bad manners, a rude and shocking eruption of that which must not be spoken or thought of in polite, tightly guarded society. To avoid controversy, to quell controversy, is often seen as a public good, a victory for etiquette, perhaps even a moral or ethical imperative.

Yet the studious, deliberate avoidance of controversy is also a whitewashing, a denial, a death threat to democracy. It is a false sterilizing and sanitizing and superficial ordering of the messy, ragged, chaotic, at times ugly processes by which a healthy democracy identifies and confronts challenges, engages in passionate debate about appropriate approaches and solutions, and arrives at something like a consensus and a broadly accepted and supported way forward. Controversy is the megaphone, the speaker's corner, the public square through which the citizenry finds and uses its voice. Controversy is the life's blood of our democracy and absolutely essential to the vibrant health of our society.

Our present age is certainly no stranger to controversy. We are consumed by fierce debates about technology, privacy, political correctness, poverty, violence, crime and policing, guns, immigration, civil and human rights, terrorism, militarism, environmental protection, and gender and racial equality. Loudly competing voices are raised every day, shouting opposing opinions, putting forth competing agendas, and summoning starkly different visions of a utopian or dystopian future. Often these voices attempt to shout the others down; there is precious little listening and considering among the cacophonous din. Yet listening and considering, too, are essential to the health of a democracy. If controversy is democracy's lusty lifeblood, respectful listening and careful thought are its higher faculties, its brain, its conscience.

Current Controversies does not shy away from or attempt to hush the loudly competing voices. It seeks to provide readers with as wide and representative as possible a range of articulate voices on any given controversy of the day, separates each one out to allow it to be heard clearly and fairly, and encourages careful listening to each of these well-crafted, thoughtfully expressed opinions, supplied by some of today's leading academics, thinkers, analysts, politicians, policy makers, economists, activists, change agents, and advocates. Only after listening to a wide range of opinions on an issue, evaluating the strengths and weaknesses of each argument, assessing how well the facts and available evidence mesh with the stated opinions and conclusions, and thoughtfully and critically examining one's own beliefs and conscience can the reader begin to arrive at his or her own conclusions and articulate his or her own stance on the spotlighted controversy.

This process is facilitated and supported in each Current Controversies volume by an introduction and chapter overviews that provide readers with the essential context they need to begin engaging with the spotlighted controversies, with the debates surrounding them, and with their own perhaps shifting or nascent opinions on them. Chapters are organized around several key questions that are answered with diverse opinions representing all points on the political spectrum. In its content, organization, and methodology, readers are encouraged to determine the authors' point of view and purpose, interrogate and analyze the various arguments and their rhetoric and structure, evaluate the arguments' strengths and weaknesses, test their claims against available facts and evidence, judge the validity of the reasoning, and bring into clearer, sharper focus the reader's own beliefs and conclusions and how they may differ from or align with those in the collection or those of classmates.

Research has shown that reading comprehension skills improve dramatically when students are provided with compelling, intriguing, and relevant "discussable" texts. The subject matter of these collections could not be more compelling, intriguing, or urgently relevant to today's students and the world they are poised to inherit. The anthologized articles also provide the basis for stimulating, lively, and passionate classroom debates. Students who are compelled to anticipate objections to their own argument and identify the flaws in those of an opponent read more carefully, think more critically, and steep themselves in relevant context, facts, and information more thoroughly. In short, using discussable text of the kind provided by every single volume in the Current Controversies series encourages close reading, facilitates reading comprehension, fosters research, strengthens critical thinking, and greatly enlivens and energizes classroom discussion and participation. The entire learning process is deepened, extended, and strengthened.

If we are to foster a knowledgeable, responsible, active, and engaged citizenry, we must provide readers with the intellectual, interpretive, and critical-thinking tools and experience necessary to make sense of the world around them and of the all-important debates and arguments that inform it. We must encourage them not to run away from or attempt to quell controversy but to embrace it in a responsible, conscientious, and thoughtful way, to sharpen and strengthen their own informed opinions by listening to and critically analyzing those of others. This series encourages respectful engagement with and analysis of current controversies and competing opinions and fosters a resulting increase in the strength and rigor of one's own opinions and stances. As such, it helps readers assume their rightful place in the public square and provides them with the skills necessary to uphold their awesome responsibility—guaranteeing the continued and future health of a vital, vibrant, and free democracy.

Introduction

> *"Much of what we see in America, what most people feel has been progress and good things, have been brought about by the existence of third parties."*
>
> —*Peter Camejo,*
> *Venezuelan American*
> *author, third-party political*
> *activist, and politician*

For the most part, two major parties dominate American politics today: the Democratic Party and the Republican Party. Politicians from these two parties tend to hold office at the municipal, state, and national level and receive far more media attention during campaigns and elections than third-party candidates. Although candidates from popular third parties are often included on the ballot in presidential elections, no third-party candidate has ever been successful at winning the presidency.[1] However, according to a September 2020 survey of American voters conducted by the political news website the Hill, 60 percent of Americans think that the US political system will only be effective if there is a viable third-party option in elections.[2] How can this incongruity between what Americans say they want and whom they choose to elect be explained?

To answer this question, it is useful to take a look at the history of the electoral system in the United States. Two parties have dominated American politics since approximately 1792, when the Federalists and Jeffersonian Republicans vied for political power.[3] Since then the parties have occasionally changed, but an electoral system that favors two parties has endured, and the two parties that currently control American politics have had a remarkably long lifespan. The Democratic Party and the Republican Party have existed as the two dominant parties since the 1850s, and although the political stances of these parties have frequently changed over time, the fundamental DNA of each party has remained the same.[4] Indeed, the last time a candidate that was not a Republican or Democrat won the presidency was in 1848, when the Whig candidate Zachary Taylor was elected.[5] Since that time, however, there have been several occasions when third-party candidates made waves in presidential elections without winning the presidency.

The most notable third-party candidate in the history of the United States is Theodore Roosevelt, who had, in fact, previously served as president when he was affiliated with the Republican Party (1901–1909).[6] In the 1912 election Roosevelt ran for president once again, but this time as a third-party candidate with the Bull Moose Party (more formally known as the Progressive Party), a new party that opposed the conservatism of Republican leadership and aimed to create a schism within the Republican Party.[7] Roosevelt was a highly successful candidate because of his name recognition, but he nonetheless lost the election by a considerable margin, having won only six states and eighty-eight electoral college votes.[8] Despite his name recognition, enthusiastic following, and a successful presidency under his belt, Roosevelt was still unable to win the election, which is a testament to the durability of both the two-party system and the Republican Party Roosevelt aimed to upend.

There are a number of systemic reasons why candidates from the two major parties tend to be so much more successful than third-party candidates. Because of the size and strength of the Republican and Democratic Parties, candidates from these parties often have significantly more resources as they campaign for office. They generally have higher campaign budgets, are able to produce more campaign ads, and have an easier time raising funds. Their candidacies tend to receive attention from major media outlets, and once a candidate is selected in the primaries for these two parties they are guaranteed a spot in presidential debates. Third-party candidates, on the other hand, are excluded from these debates unless polls indicate they have at least 15 percent of the public's support ahead of these debates, a daunting and arguably arbitrary threshold for third-party candidates to reach.[9] States each have their own filing requirements and deadlines dictated in ballot access laws, so in some occasions third-party candidates will not even end up on the ballot in certain states.[10]

Perhaps even more significant than the issues of exposure faced by third-party candidates is the nature of the electoral process in the United States itself. This is because almost all US elections are conducted as a plurality vote with single-member districts, which means this is a winner-takes-all system in which voters cast one vote and the candidate that receives the most votes wins the election, regardless of how close the election may be.[11] Some argue that ranked choice voting—a system in which voters would rank candidates according to preference—would give third parties a better shot, but until this occurs it will likely continue to be a significant challenge for a third-party candidate to win an election.[12]

Despite these challenges, third parties persist in American politics. Though there are numerous third parties that are currently active in the United States, the two major third parties that will be discussed in this volume are the Libertarian Party and the Green Party. The socialist movement will also factor into the conversation—in particular the Democratic Socialists of America (DSA)—though this movement differs from more conventional third parties.

The Libertarian Party is the third-largest party in the United States, after the Democratic and Republican Parties.[13] It was founded in 1971 with the intention of limiting the powers of the government, reducing or eliminating taxes whenever possible, and protecting personal liberties.[14] The Green Party got its start in Europe in the early 1970s as an anti-nuclear, pro-peace environmental movement called the European Greens, but it had a great impact on the US environmental movement of the 1970s and ultimately led to the formation of the US Green Party in 1984.[15] As the name implies, the party is focused on promoting "green"—or environmentally sustainable—policies, as well as progressive policies that support racial, gender, and economic equality.

The socialist movement has a long history in the United States. It took root in America in the 1830s with the formation of socialist utopian experimental communities, but its era of greatest prominence was in the early twentieth century, a period characterized by Eugene Debs's candidacy as a socialist candidate in five presidential elections between 1900 and 1920, as well as the election of various socialist candidates across the country during this era.[16] During the Cold War (1947–1991), propagandistic ad campaigns ensured socialism was conflated with communism and deemed "un-American," which has made it difficult for socialist candidates to succeed in elections ever since.[17] The most notable socialist organization involved in contemporary US politics is the Democratic Socialists of America (DSA), which originated in 1982 after the merger of two different socialist organizations.[18] The DSA promotes the radical transformation of the government and economy to promote a more equitable society, and rather than operating as a separate party it is an organizing movement that supports the Democratic Party by endorsing candidates that align with their values and helping impact the party platform.[19] Notable candidates and politicians that are affiliated with the DSA include Bernie Sanders, Alexandria Ocasio-Cortez, and Rashida Tlaib.

Although the path to election is often difficult to maneuver for third-party candidates, third-party supporters should not be entirely without hope. It is useful to consider the different ways to define success for third parties beyond winning a presidential election. In a number of cases, third parties have played a role in impacting the platforms of the two major parties. The support for Green Party candidates like Jill Stein in the 2016 presidential election and Ralph Nader in the 2000 election—which some believe "spoiled" the election for the Democratic candidates—pushed the Democratic Party to adopt more green policies in their platform to win over supporters. Likewise, although Libertarian candidates are generally not considered frontrunners in presidential races, Libertarian interest groups, donors, and lobbyists play a behind-the-scenes role in elections.[20] DSA-affiliated candidates and politicians like Bernie Sanders and Alexandria Ocasio-Cortez have helped push the Democratic Party farther left, pressuring Democratic candidates to support more progressive policies. Furthermore, third-party candidates are considerably more successful at the municipal and state level. As of August 2020, 232 Libertarians held elected offices across the country.[21] Following the 2018 mid-term election, eleven DSA members were elected to state legislatures, two were elected to the US House of Representatives, and more than a dozen were elected to city councils across the US.[22] These trends indicate that third parties could be effective at implementing change on a more local level.

The viewpoints in *Current Controversies: Libertarians, Socialists, and Other Third Parties* examine differing perspectives on the historical and contemporary role of third parties in US politics. It considers the factors that impact their electability, potential ways to create fairer elections, and the ways in which these parties can affect politics even without winning presidential elections. Ultimately, readers will be empowered to form opinions on the nature of US electoral politics and potential solutions to the issues the American electorate faces today.

Notes

1. Julia Foodman, "A History of Third Party and Independent Presidential Candidates," FairVote, July 16, 2019, https://www.fairvote.org/a_history_of_independent_presidential_candidates.

2. Gabriela Schulte, "Poll: 60 Percent of Voters Say a Viable Third Party Is Needed to Have an Effective Political System," the Hill, September 18, 2020, https://thehill.com/hilltv/what-americas-thinking/517088-poll-60-percent-of-voters-say-a-viable-third-party-is-needed-to.

3. Marc Horger, "Breaking Up Is Hard to Do: America's Love Affair with the Two-Party System," Origins, July 2013, http://origins.osu.edu/article/breaking-hard-do -americas-love-affair-two-party-system.

4. Eric Black, "Why the Same Two Parties Dominate Our Two-Party System," *MinnPost*, October 8, 2012, https://www.minnpost.com/eric-black-ink/2012/10 /why-same-two-parties-dominate-our-two-party-system/.

5. Ibid.

6. Marc Horger, "Breaking Up Is Hard to Do: America's Love Affair with the Two-Party System," Origins, July 2013, http://origins.osu.edu/article/breaking-hard-do -americas-love affair-two-party-system.

7. "Bull Moose Party," *Encyclopaedia Britannica*, https://www.britannica.com/topic /Bull-Moose-Party.

8. Daniel Bush, "What Would It Take for a Third-Party Candidate to Take It to the White House?" *PBS NewsHour*, September 25, 2016, https://www.pbs.org /newshour/politics/americas-off-love-affair-third-party-candidates.

9. Katie McNally, "The Third-Party Impact on American Politics," *UVA Today*, August 3, 2016, https://news.virginia.edu/content/third-party-impact-american -politics.

10. "Ballot Access for Major and Minor Party Candidates," Ballotpedia, https:// ballotpedia.org/Ballot_access_for_major_and_minor_party_candidates.

11. Eric Black, "Why the Same Two Parties Dominate Our Two-Party System," *MinnPost*, October 8, 2012, https://www.minnpost.com/eric-black-ink/2012/10 /why-same-two-parties-dominate-our-two-party-system/.

12. Julia Foodman, "A History of Third Party and Independent Presidential Candidates," FairVote, July 16, 2019, https://www.fairvote.org/a_history_of_ independent_presidential_candidates.

13. "About the Libertarian Party," Libertarian National Committee, Inc., https://www .lp.org/about/.

14. Ibid.

15. The Association of State Green Parties, "Green Party History," *PBS NewsHour*, 2000, https://www.pbs.org/newshour/spc/bb/politics/jan-june00 /green_history.html.

16. Joey Lautrup, "Bernie Sanders' New Hampshire Victory Is a Big Deal for Socialism in America. Here's What to Know About the History of the Idea," *Time*, February 12, 2020, https://time.com/5762312/bernie-sanders-socialism-america/.

17. Oana Godeanu-Kenworthy, "How Socialism Became Un-American Through the Ad Council's Propaganda Campaigns," the Conversation, February 27, 2020, https://theconversation.com/how-socialism-became-un-american-through-the -ad-councils-propaganda-campaigns-132335.

18. "A History of Democratic Socialists of America 1971–2017," Democratic Socialists of America, July 2017, https://www.dsausa.org/about-us/history/.

19. "What Is Democratic Socialism?" Democratic Socialists of America, https://www
.dsausa.org/about-us/what-is-democratic-socialism/#party.

20. Olivier Lewis and Jeffrey Michels, "Primary Primers: How Libertarians Could Be
the Kingmakers of the 2020 Presidential Election," LSE US Centre, November 15,
2019, https://blogs.lse.ac.uk/usappblog/2019/11/15/how-libertarians-could-be
-the-kingmakers-of-the-2020-presidential-election/.

21. "Libertarian Party," Ballotpedia, https://ballotpedia.org/Libertarian_Party.

22. Elaine Godfrey, "Thousands of Americans Have Become Socialists Since March,"
Atlantic, May 14, 2020, https://www.theatlantic.com/politics/archive/2020/05/dsa
-growing-during-coronavirus/611599/.

CHAPTER 1

Have Third Parties Always Been Active in the United States?

Overview: The Role of Third Parties in US Politics Is Up for Debate

Kristina Nwazota

Kristina Nwazota is a senior online communications officer for the World Bank Africa region. She previously was an online international editor for NewsHour.

Despite an active political presence, only two parties—the Democrats and Republicans—dominate the modern American political process, between them fielding all of the candidates that have become president since the mid-1800s.

Why, in a democracy, do only two parties dominate? What of the 52 other parties, many of which have contributed ideas and policies that have become mainstays of American political life and law? The answer, according to historians and scholars, is the political process that has relegated third parties to the sidelines and the nature of the parties themselves.

The Green Party, Reform Party, Libertarians, Constitution Party and Natural Law Party represent the most active third parties currently in the United States. All of these parties have fielded presidential candidates in the last several elections.

Ralph Nader, an independent candidate in the 2004 presidential race, made his name as a consumer advocate and as the two-time presidential nominee of the Green Party. As the Green Party candidate in 2000, he gained more than 2 million votes, coming in third behind Al Gore and George W. Bush. But controversy marred the Green Party accomplishment. Democrats blamed Nader for causing Gore's defeat by siphoning off votes simply by his presence in the race.

The Green Party platform centers largely on the environment, while Libertarians, which make up the third largest political party in the country and the oldest of the third parties, believe in a reduced role of the government. They maintain that the government should serve only as a form of protection for citizens. Although no Libertarian Party candidate has ever become president, several of its members hold elected office in state and local government.

The American Taxpayers Party, which changed its name to the Constitution Party in 2000, advocates a strict interpretation of the Constitution and more power for states and localities. Its most popular candidate Howard Phillips ran for office in 1992 but received less than 1 percent of the vote.

Third Parties Success & Influence

The most successful of the third parties in any one election was the Reform Party, which in 1992 nominated Texas billionaire Ross Perot as its candidate for president. Perot ran on a platform that advocated reducing the federal budget deficit, an issue previously ignored in elections but one that would become a major part of almost every presidential campaign since. Perot received 19 percent of the vote.

"[H]e was the first candidate really in a big way to float the idea that the deficit was a bad thing," said historian Michael Beschloss. "By the time Bill Clinton was elected that fall, if he had not done something about the deficit he would have been in big trouble and that was largely Ross Perot's doing."

Third parties have had a major influence on US policy and political debate despite their minor presence in Congress—currently only one US senator and one member of the House of Representatives is an independent.

In the late 1800s and early 1900s, the Socialists popularized the women's suffrage movement. They advocated for child labor laws in 1904 and, along with the Populist Party, introduced the notion of a 40-hour work week, which led to the Fair Labor Standards Act of 1938.

"What happens is third parties act as a gadfly," said Sean Wilentz, director of the American Studies program at Princeton

University. "There'll be an issue that's being neglected or that is being purposely excluded from national debate because neither party wants to face the political criticism that it would bring. A classic example was slavery."

"It's a kind of bitter sweetness," he added. "[Third parties] are the ones that raise the issues that no one wants to raise and in the process they change the political debate and even policy, but they themselves as a political force, they disappear."

Obstacles Third Parties Face

In fact, American voters have not elected a third party president since Abraham Lincoln when the then-minority Republican Party beat the Whigs and the Democrats in 1860 on the anti-slavery platform. Voters often worry that a vote for a third party candidate is "wasted" since he or she is unlikely to win.

Also, according to Beschloss, third parties often organize around a single personality or a single issue and that can lead to less popularity among voters.

Perhaps the most significant of the obstacles facing third party candidates is the winner-take-all system. In most states, the presidential candidate with the highest percentage of votes gets all the state's electoral votes.

"There's no reward for second place," said John F. Bibby, University of Wisconsin professor and co-author of the book *Two Parties—Or More? The American Party System*. "With a single elected president if you're going to have a chance to win the states, which are all awarded on a winner-take-all basis, again you don't have a chance. The incentive is to form broad-based parties that have a chance to win in the Electoral College."

In his book, Bibby and co-author L. Sandy Maisel point to Ross Perot in 1992, who had widespread appeal but not enough to win a state completely.

Third party candidates also are at a disadvantage because of federal campaign finance laws, rules that dictate who can enter presidential debates, and a lack of media attention.

"It's very difficult for third parties to get media coverage," Bibby said. "In Nader's last run, the questions they asked him 'Why are you running?' (came) all the time, not about the substance of his campaign."

In addition, a significant amount of paperwork is required to become a viable candidate. When Ralph Nader announced in February 2004 that he would seek the presidential nomination, he was required to collect 1.5 million signatures in all states to appear on the ballot. Deadlines for those signatures began as early as May 2004.

Campaign finance rules say that a political party can only get government funding to run a race if it received a certain percentage of votes from the previous election. Often this leaves third party candidates to fund their own campaigns. With less media coverage, the candidates are left to find other means of exposure to raise the millions of dollars it takes to run a successful campaign.

Political analyst and comedian Bill Maher expressed disbelief that Americans would willingly accept only two choices for president. "It's silly," he said, "that a country that prides itself on choice allows only two."

Others argue that the two-party system is one that promotes stability by avoiding a more divided government.

"The US Constitution was written long before parties came into being. The framers distrusted parties," Sean Wilentz said. "But once parties did emerge, the system that the framers set up tended to encourage coalitions that fight it out and those coalitions tend to be two in number."

The Democrats and the Republicans, according to Wilentz, over the decades have come to represent two basic and contrasting ideas about how politics and policy should be run.

"[The Republicans] are very much a conservative party and the Democrats are very much a liberal party, and I think that they stand because more and more they have come to represent those two points of view," he said.

Bibby agrees. "It's the nature of American society and the beliefs of Americans in that we have relatively few on the extreme," he said. "Most Americans are relatively moderate and they can operate comfortably within a system where one party is slightly to the right and the other slightly to the left. They don't see any great need for an alternative.

In either case, this year's presidential election promises to continue the trend. Analysts favor the Republican or Democratic Party to win, and of the 81 other candidates hoping to enter the race, the public will probably only know the name of a very select few.

In Reality, the US Political System Does Not Neatly Break Down into Two Parties

Domenico Montanaro

Domenico Montanaro is a senior political editor and correspondent for NPR's Washington desk.

There is a political crackup happening in America. There remain two major political parties in this country, but there are stark fissures within each. There seem to be roughly at least four stripes of politics today—the pragmatic left (think: Obama-Clinton, the left-of-center establishment Democrats), the pragmatic right (the Bush-McCain-Bob Corker Republican), the populist right (Trump's America) and the populist left (Bernie Sanders liberals).

But a new political typology out Tuesday from the Pew Research Center, based on surveys of more than 5,000 adults conducted over the summer, goes even deeper. It finds eight distinct categories of political ideology (nine if you include "bystanders," those not engaged with politics).

They are as follows, from most conservative to most liberal (in part based on how many of them crossover between the two major parties. It also mostly tracks with their approval or Trump):

1. Core Conservatives—13 percent of the general public
2. Country First Conservatives—6 percent
3. Market Skeptic Republicans—12 percent
4. New Era Enterprisers—11 percent
5. Devout and Diverse—9 percent
6. Disaffected Democrats—14 percent
7. Opportunity Democrats—12 percent
8. Solid Liberals—16 percent

While the Solid Liberals and Core Conservatives make up less than a third of the total population, they make up almost half of the most politically engaged. Because of that, they have an outsize influence in US politics.

They are also, predictably, the most interested in the 2018 election. There's a stark drop off in interest in the midterms among any other group, and that points to yet again a midterm election where the most activist dominate and there's a drop in turnout from a presidential year.

Meanwhile, Pew also identified a sizable portion of the American population that are essentially political "bystanders." They're not engaged with politics, not registered to vote, young and majority-minority. And there's a lot of them—8 percent of the population, or roughly 20 million people.

Overall, Pew sums up its findings, in a new 150-page report, this way:

> Nearly a year after Donald Trump was elected president, the Republican coalition is deeply divided on such major issues as immigration, America's role in the world and the fundamental fairness of the US economic system.
>
> The Democratic coalition is largely united in staunch opposition to President Trump. Yet, while Trump's election has triggered a wave of political activism within the party's sizable liberal bloc, the liberals' sky-high political energy is not nearly as evident among other segments in the Democratic base. And Democrats also are internally divided over US global involvement, as well as some religious and social issues.

Here's how the eight groups break down:

Republican leaners—four groups

1. Core Conservatives

13 percent of the country, 31 percent of Republicans, 43 percent of politically engaged Republicans. They are, as Pew describes:

- Male dominated and financially comfortable
- In favor of smaller government and lower corporate tax rates

- Of the belief that the US economic system is fair—four-fifths don't believe the government can afford to do more for needy Americans and that blacks who can't get ahead are responsible for their own condition
- Believers in US involvement in the global economy. You might call them "globalists."
- Not very socially conservative—a majority don't think immigrants are a burden and just over a third believes homosexuality should be discouraged by society.

And yet this group approves strongly of Trump. Fully 93 percent approve of the president's job performance, the highest of any group. It's even more than the Country First category, and you'll see why that might be surprising in the next section.

This could simply be the product of Core Conservatives being more politically engaged generally—and more likely to wear the "GOP" T-shirt.

2. Country First

6 percent of the country, 14 percent of Republicans, 14 percent of politically engaged Republicans. They are:

- Older and less educated than other Republican-leaning voters
- Unhappy with the direction of the country
- Nationalist—they believe the country is too open to immigrants and that Americans risk "losing our identity as a nation" because of it
- Protectionist—they don't like the US involved around the world and they think immigrants are a burden
- Not of the belief that the government should do more to help the needy (70 percent) and they believe that blacks who can't get ahead are responsible for their own condition (76 percent)
- Socially conservative—they believe that homosexuality should be discouraged by society (70 percent)
- Populist—they're less likely than most other Republicans to believe the US economic system is fair to most Americans

3. Market Skeptic Republicans

12 percent of the country, 22 percent of Republicans, but only 17 percent of the most politically engaged. They are:

- Populist—they believe banks and financial institutions have a negative effect on the direction of the country; 94 percent believe the economic system favors the powerful. That is much closer to Solid Liberals than Core Conservatives. And they do not believe that US economy is fair to most—just 5 percent think so. This is a major distinction between them and the other GOP-leaning groups.
- In favor of raising taxes on corporations and small businesses—the only GOP-leaning group to feel that way
- Of the belief that government can't afford to do more to help needy Americans. A strong majority (58 percent) says so, but they are the least likely Republican leaning group to feel that way.
- Of the belief that blacks who can't get ahead are responsible for their own condition.
- Fairly socially liberal—just 31 percent believe homosexuality should be discouraged by society
- Somewhat protectionist, though less than Country First Republicans—they are split on US involvement around the globe

4. New Era Enterprisers

11 percent of the country, 17 percent of Republicans, 16 percent of the most engaged Republicans. They are:

- Youngest of the Republican-leaning categories, with an average age of 47
- Optimistic about the country—they are the most likely group to believe the next generation will be better off
- Pro-business and trade (they're globalists, too), of the belief that the economy is generally fair to most Americans (75 percent say so)

- Of the belief that being involved around the globe is good for markets
- Socially liberal—believing immigrants are not a burden and that homosexuality should not be discouraged by society
- Somewhat more diverse—two-thirds are white, but that's the lowest of all other GOP-leaning groups

Democratic Leaners—Four Groups

5. Devout and Diverse

9 percent of the country, 11 percent of Democrats, just 6 percent of the most politically engaged. They are:

- Majority-minority, struggling financially, older and the least educated of the Democratic-leaning categories. Just 15 percent have college degrees.
- Very religious. Nearly two-thirds believe it is necessary to believe in God to be moral and have good values.
- Politically mixed. A quarter are Republicans. It's the category with the most crossover.
- The strongest Democratic-leaning group to believe the US should pay more attention at home than to problems overseas
- Largely pro-business and don't believe government regulation is necessary to protect the public's interest
- Perhaps unsurprisingly, it's the most pro-Trump Democratic group (though 60 percent still disapprove of him), but...
- Of the belief that government should provide safety nets like everyone having health care and that the country needs to still make changes to advance racial equality

6. Disaffected Democrats

14 percent of the country, 23 percent of Democrats, 11 percent of the most politically engaged.

The label doesn't have to do with their disaffection with the Democratic Party. They actually regard the Democratic Party very favorably. But rather they're disaffected with government (most of them say government is "wasteful and inefficient"); politics generally (most believe voting does not give them a say in how government runs); and the direction of the country.

They're also:

- Majority-minority, lower educated, financially stressed—and fairly young (with an average age of 44)
- Anti-Trump, pro-social safety net and believe the US needs to continue making changes to affect racial equality
- Split, however, on whether hard work can help you get ahead
- Not of the belief government regulation is necessary to protect the public interest
- Of the belief that the US should pay more attention to problems at home

7. Opportunity Democrats

12 percent of the country, 20 percent of Democrats, 13 percent of the most politically engaged. They are:

- Majority white and working-to-middle-class, and only a third have college degrees
- Largely liberal when it comes to the role of government, strongly in disapproval of Trump and two-thirds believe the country needs to do more to give blacks equal rights to whites (though that's the lowest of the four Democratic-leaning groups), but...
- Very much in disagreement with other Democratic-leaning groups about the ability to make it in the US through hard work. They believe strongly that you can. But they are not protectionist. They believe in global engagement.

8. Solid Liberals

16 percent of the country, 33 percent of Democrats, 25 percent of the most politically engaged. They are:

- Largely white, well-educated and comfortable financially
- Young (average age of only 44)

- Unified, almost unanimously in their disapproval of Trump (99 percent disapprove). And they are activist about it—half say they have contributed to a candidate or campaign in the past year. For context, just a third of Core Conservatives say the same. Four-in-10 Solid Liberals say they've participated in a protest against Trump's policies.
- Unified in their belief that government has the responsibility to make sure all Americans have health care and have a strong sense of racial justice. There is near-unanimous agreement among this group that the country needs to continue making changes to give blacks equal rights with whites.
- Of the belief that hard work and determination are no guarantee of success in the United States. Nearly three-quarters of this group says so, and this is an area where they largely differ from the other three Democratic groups as well as the Republican-leaning categories.
- Strongly of the belief that it's necessary to regulate businesses to protect the public interest, another area where they differ with half of the Democratic-leaning categories and all of the Republican-leaning ones
- Very much globalists. Very few, just one-in-10, believe the US should pay less attention overseas and focus more on problems at home. That is a major difference with two of the Democratic-leaning categories and three of the Republican-leaning ones.
- Largely nonreligious. Just 9 percent believe it's necessary to believe in God to be moral and have good values.

America Has a Long History of Progressive Socialism

Jo-Ann Mort

Jo-Ann Mort is a writer who frequently writes about Israel for various publications in the US, the UK, and Israel, including the Guardian. *She is co-author of* Our Hearts Invented a Place: Can Kibbutzim Survive in Today's Israel?

Attempting to scare swing voters onto their side in the US presidential campaign, the McCain-Palin ticket has taken to throwing around the term "socialism" to define Barack Obama's argument in support of progressive taxation. The latter will create more equality, or in Obama's own words, "spread the wealth around." Yet while Obama, with billionaire businessman Warren Buffett and former US Federal Reserve chairman Paul Volcker among his top financial advisers, may support a more equitable America, he is no socialist.

Which isn't to say that an Obama administration couldn't inspire socialist policies or attitudes. And to my mind, that's nothing to be ashamed of. As someone whose secular "rabbis" were socialist thinkers, like the late writer and activist Michael Harrington and the literary and political thinker and Yiddishist Irving Howe, I find it intriguing and inspiring to hear this debate—though not as it's being framed by McCain.

There has long been a progressive, home-grown socialist tradition in the US, even if in recent decades it has waned—until perhaps now. At the turn of the 20th century, it was the middle-American socialism of Eugene Debs, whose Indiana, trade-union roots helped him lure hundreds of thousands of passionate urban Jewish immigrants to his cause. During the 1950s and 1960s, it was the urbane, religiously inspired socialism of Norman Thomas,

A Modern-Day Eugene Debs," by Jo-Ann Mort, Guardian News & Media Limited, October 29, 2008. Reprinted by permission.

an ordained Presbyterian minister from Ohio, who served as the moral voice of a nation, famously telling protesters in one of the earliest demonstrations against the Vietnam war: "We have come to cleanse the [American] flag, not to burn it."

Harrington took his inspiration from Dorothy Day's Catholic Worker movement. His 1962 book *The Other America* inspired another president—Lyndon Johnson—to declare a "war" on poverty. Harrington died in 1989, but his writings are as prescient today as they were when he wrote them. He sometimes called his philosophy "republican socialism," harkening back to the founding principles of the nation, when the US broke from the English monarchy to create a republic of citizens, rather than be subjects of the crown.

Years ago, I was given a framed broadside of socialist inspiration as a gift from a family member of another well-regarded American socialist, Sidney Hillman. A rabbi's grandson, Hillman came from Russia to America, founded the Amalgamated Clothing Workers union and was a key player in domestic politics during Franklin Roosevelt's New Deal. Today, these words of Harrington hang above my desk:

> I insist that the political, social and economic development of modern society points socialism toward an ethical, multiclass, and decentralised conception of its goal based on the democratisation of the workplace and the creation of new forms of community, both within the nation and throughout the world. That vision has a remarkable continuity with the basic republican values that derives from both the French and the American revolutions.

Obama's stance is significant, not because he has proclaimed allegiance to socialist ideology—he hasn't—but rather because he is expressing support for notions of social solidarity and interdependency and government intervention akin to European social democracy. Surely the majority of Americans don't link these values to any kind of socialist strain. Unlike Europe, socialism and social democracy are not even part of the American political scene.

But Americans are searching for a vision of society different from our present one. That's why the Democratic candidate has been speaking to overflow crowds throughout the campaign. Obama has ignited a generation that may know little about the grand political arguments of an earlier era, but that feels—and "feels" is the operative word—that something is terribly wrong.

Americans are hungry for an end to the inequality and social meanness that have exemplified the Bush years. With record-breaking gaps between the rich and the poor, driven by policies that emphasised privatisation, deregulation and lack of government supports, the America the next president will inherit was in deep financial distress even before the recent global financial crash. But we have also been in emotional distress. As we privatised the economy, so too, we privatised social life and the public sphere. And that's where the socialist model is a useful one. It's about engaging people in civic life, recreating a public square that is applicable to a 21st-century world.

American socialism was always more about trade union syndicalism, religious values, communitarianism and a profound belief in small "d" democracy, small "r" republicanism. It was also staunchly anti-authoritarian. (The significant exception to this, of course, was the American Communist party, which drew its ideology from an authoritarian model.)

"Can we really create a space for personal and community freedom in a modern society?" Harrington wondered. "No one can be sure. All we can say with confidence is that if such freedom is to come into existence, it will be the result of new global structures of solidarity and justice. Which is to say, of socialism."

On November 5, when the world wakes up to a new American president, perhaps it will have its answer.

Third-Party Candidates Have the Power to Change Election Outcomes

Daniel P. Franklin, Abigail C. Bowen, and Judd Thornton

Daniel P. Franklin is an associate professor of political science at Georgia State University, where Abigail C. Bowen is a PhD student of political science and Judd Thornton is an assistant professor of political science.

G reen Party candidate Jill Stein does not see herself as a spoiler in the 2016 presidential race.

Her voters, Stein claims, would not have come to the polls had she not been in the race.

But what if Stein were wrong and she didn't bring new voters to the polls? The number of votes Stein got in Michigan and Wisconsin exceeded the gap between Clinton and Trump in those states. If you assume that Stein voters were more liberal than conservative and therefore more likely to support Clinton than Trump, Stein could have been a spoiler in those two states.

Of course, winning Michigan and Wisconsin would not have given Clinton the presidency. But the question of whether third-party candidates expand the electorate has important implications in last year's election—and in presidential elections in general.

We are scholars of politics and the presidency, but you don't need to be an expert to know that a shift or addition of just a few thousand votes in one or two key states can determine the outcome of a presidential election. In other words, a handful of voters in the right place at the right time can truly change the course of American history.

"Are Third-Party Candidates Spoilers? What Voting Data Reveal," by Daniel P. Franklin, Abigail C. Bowen, and Judd Thornton, The Conversation, January 18, 2017. https://theconversation.com/are-third-party-candidates-spoilers-what-voting-data-reveal-71065. Licensed under CC BY-ND 4.0.

And so, we decided to test the notion that third-party candidates increase turnout in presidential elections.

Third-Party Candidacies in History

To start, we collected voter turnout data going back to the election of 1868. That election was the first after the Civil War and represents the earliest days of the modern two-party system.

We looked at how voter turnout interacted with the voting performance of third-party candidacies. We took into consideration the expansion of the voting franchise through the 15th Amendment, which granted universal male suffrage; the 19th Amendment, which extended the vote to women; the 26th Amendment, which lowered the voting age to 18; and the Voting Rights Act. We also compensated for historical and demographic trends.

We found that not only do third-party candidacies fail to increase turnout, they are actually associated with a statistically significant reduction in turnout. Put simply, fewer people vote in elections in which third-party candidates receive a substantial portion of the vote.

Potential Causes for Decreased Turnout

Be careful. That's not the same thing as saying third-party candidates reduce turnout.

Establishing causality here is a little bit tricky. To say that one thing is related to something else is not to say that one thing causes the other. You may have a cup of coffee every morning, but drinking coffee doesn't cause the sun to rise.

We think it's unlikely that third-party candidacies actually dampen turnout. Rather, we believe that their success represents dissatisfaction with the choices offered by the two major parties. Voters are then less likely to turn out, and those who do are more likely to choose a third-party candidate.

We would like to test that theory by examining voter attitudes at the individual level. This would involve isolating and comparing the voting behavior of third-party voters with the general voting population in large-scale national surveys such as the American National Election Study.

In the meantime, there are some much more plausible explanations for our results. It may be that third parties encourage the turnout of new voters—as Stein claims—but that what is happening at the same time is that the major party candidates dampen turnout even more. That scenario seems unlikely to us simply because it involves too many moving parts.

The more likely explanation, we believe, is that there is an existing pool of habitual voters and that third-party candidates draw their support from voters who would have gone to the polls anyhow.

This hypothesis is supported by research that suggests the decision to vote is not necessarily motivated in the same way as the choice between candidates. Most voters first make the decision to vote, and only then choose for whom to vote. Most voters go to the polls out of a sense of obligation and patriotism, not in support of an individual candidate. These voters who are motivated out of habit or by a sense of civic duty are what we call habitual voters.

The number of habitual voters may vary marginally according to the rules of the game. Making voter registration more difficult or elections less competitive tends to dampen turnout.

It is also the case that expanding the right to vote has had the perverse effect of appearing to lower voter turnout. As the pool of eligible voters increases, the turnout percentage decreases.

On the other hand, our results show that the Voting Rights Act had the effect of significantly increasing turnout because it expanded participation within an existing voter pool.

But the overriding fact is that when controlling for the expansion of the voting pool, turnout does not vary widely from one election to the next. That suggests that most voters go to the polls because they want to vote, not because they are motivated by any particular candidate. The one exception to this rule appears to be Ross Perot's candidacy in 1992. But the one thing that distinguished his candidacy was the US$100 million of his own money he had to spend. By way of contrast, Jill Stein raised and spent about $3.5 million in the latest campaign cycle.

In the 2000 election, Ralph Nader's candidacy affected the outcome in Florida. Nader campaigned actively in Florida and received about 97,000 votes. The winner in Florida between Bush and Gore was determined by less than a thousand. As a result, the Nader campaign swung the election in a direction that from his and his supporters' perspective was less favorable than the election of Al Gore.

Most voters anticipate this problem and abandon third-party candidacies as the election approaches. However, those who insist on voting for third-party candidates are often actually voting against their own preference.

Of course, third-party candidacies can promote ideas out of the mainstream. However, our research suggests that voters need to think long and hard about voting for a third-party candidate—especially if they live in competitive states.

The Two-Party System Is an Efficient Way to Represent the Values of American Voters

J. J. McCullough

J. J. McCullough is a columnist for National Review Online and for the global opinions section of the Washington Post.

Bashing the American two-party system never goes out of style, but at present it seems trendier than usual. A populist age begets fresh animosity for partisan traditions.

In the *New York Times*, David Brooks portrays the system as something contrary to the diversity of American life. "There are over 6,000 breweries in America," he complains, "but when it comes to our politics, we get to choose between Soviet Refrigerator Factory A and Soviet Refrigerator Factory B." In a column entitled "The Third Party Option," he makes the case for an explicitly "radical" presidential candidate with unorthodox opinions capable of outshining the other two. Fellow conservative Henry Olsen echoes similar sentiments, arguing for a "National Party," bearing a unique platform whose understandings of life, liberty, and the state transcend the conventional constraints of American partisanship.

On the opposite end, *Jacobin*'s Seth Ackerman argues for a new leftist party defined by structure and discipline. Like many on the hard left, he bemoans a Democratic party indifferent to socialism, but he considers this fate primarily a byproduct of America's insufficiently "stringent" party hierarchies. Ackerman is encouraged by leftists such as Bernie Sanders and Alexandria Ocasio-Cortez, who are tied to organizations such as Democratic Socialists of America, which impose more "consistent ideological and programmatic coherence." He regards this as one of the most admirable qualities of political parties in other nations as well and envies them for it.

"America's Two-Party System Is a Triumph of Democracy," by J. J. McCullough, *National Review*, August 14, 2018. Reprinted by permission.

But the structure of America's parties makes them far less unrepresentative of American public opinion than they are charged as being. If American parties seem unsatisfying to their critics, those critics should redirect their displeasure to the voters who select the men and women who lead them.

American parties are remarkably open things. Their most significant hiring decisions are made by the Americans who choose to vote in their primaries. That Democratic and Republican politicians often proceed to discriminate against lesser parties with ballot-access laws and so forth can't hide the reality that even a party rigging things in its favor doesn't really know on whose behalf he is rigging in the long term.

Following the rise of open-to-anyone primaries in the latter half of the last century, the American party system has been colonized by voters in a way that manifests the cleavages of American civilization. There is a progressive party shaped by the culture and norms of America's great egalitarian causes, including the civil-rights movement and organized labor, and a conservative one defined by its defense of the great American institutions, including business and religion.

It is fashionable to attest that America's two-party system is arbitrary in its division, that the complexities of American life cannot be sorted into two take-it-or-leave-it bundles. Obviously, there exist Americans whose beliefs straddle or transcend the stereotypical norms of our partisan divide—the pot-smoking Evangelical, the gay uber-capitalist, etc. But as thinkers such as Yuval Levin, Roger Scruton, Jordan Peterson, and others have discussed at length, the depth of our contemporary Left–Right divide is rooted in a fundamental conflict over questions of liberty, law, and culture. Most of us instinctively identify with one argument or the other.

Take a look at those celebrated countries boasting "more" parties than America. In practice, their buffet often consists of little more than a slew of secessionist movements, personality cults, and archaic legacy parties kept alive by inertia. To the degree that more philosophically grounded parties exist, politics often takes the form of battles to eliminate redundancy, as has been in view recently with the crumbling of Europe's social democrats as voters migrate to farther-left options.

The American party system is far more elegant and efficient thanks to strong voter control. Today, most Republicans are conservative in a particular way because there exists a sizable faction of American voters who want this style of conservatism. Most Democrats are progressive in the way they are because there exists a similarly ample electorate demanding it. There are areas of the country whose tastes differ somewhat, yet it is the brilliance of the American party system that these people, pro-life Democrats, anti-gun Republicans, whatever, are permitted to hold influence—but, and here is the critical stipulation—in proportion to their base of support.

There is nothing to stop any American with some wonderfully esoteric philosophy from winning a major-party nomination. They simply have to pick a brand and mobilize enough voters to win a primary. Donald Trump, Susan Collins, Joe Manchin, Rand Paul, Bob Casey, John McCain, and other free spirits have proven it's entirely possible to pull in new people and revise their parties' identities, though at some point their creativity will hit the confines of the Left–Right sociocultural divide that voters seem determined to enforce.

It's fine to believe that American politicians are not where Americans want them—to assume that Democrats crave more Marxism, or that Republicans want less traditionalism, or some wilder theory. But there has always been an exceedingly easy way to test this thesis, a test very few party systems on earth are willing to extend to political eccentrics and dissidents: Run, and see what the voters say.

The Two-Party System Has a Strong Hold on US Politics

Tom Murse

Tom Murse is a former political reporter. He is now the managing editor of the daily newspaper LNP *and the weekly political paper the* Caucus.

The two party system is firmly rooted in American politics and has been since the first organized political movements emerged in the late 1700s. The two party system in the United States is now dominated by the Republicans and the Democrats. But through history the Federalists and the Democratic-Republicans, then the Democrats and the Whigs, have represented opposing political ideologies and campaigned against each other for seats at the local, state and federal levels.

No third-party candidate has ever been elected to the White House, and very few have won seats in either the House of Representatives or the US Senate. The most notable modern exception to the two party system is US Sen. Bernie Sanders of Vermont, a socialist whose campaign for the 2016 Democratic presidential nomination invigorated liberal members of the party. The closest any independent presidential candidate has come to being elected to the White House was billionaire Texan Ross Perot, who won 19 percent of the popular vote in the 1992 election.

So why is the two party system unbreakable in the United States? Why do Republicans and Democrats hold a lock on elected offices at all levels of government? Is there any hope for a third party to emerge or independent candidates to gain traction despite election laws that make it difficult for them to get on the ballot, organize and raise money?

"The Two Party System in American Politics," by Tom Murse, Dotdash Publishing Family, March 10, 2018. Reprinted by permission.

Here are four reasons the two party system is here to stay for a long, long time.

1. Most Americans Are Affiliated with a Major Party

Yes, this is the most obvious explanation for why the two party system remains solidly intact: Voters want it that way. A majority of Americans is registered with the Republican and the Democratic parties, and that's been true throughout modern history, according to public-opinion surveys conducted by the Gallup organization. It is true that the portion of voters who now consider themselves independent of either major party is larger than either the Republican and Democratic blocs alone. But those independent voters are disorganized and rarely reach a consensus on the many third-party candidates; instead, most independents tend to lean toward one of the major parties come election time, leaving only a small portion of truly independent, third-party voters.

2. Our Election System Favors a Two Party System

The American system of electing representatives at all levels of government makes it almost impossible for a third party to take root. We have what are known as "single-member districts" in which there is only one victor. The winner of the popular vote in all 435 congressional districts, US Senate races and state legislative contests takes office, and the electoral losers get nothing. This winner-take-all method fosters a two-party system and differs dramatically from "proportional representation" elections in European democracies.

Duverger's Law, named for the French sociologist Maurice Duverger, states that "a majority vote on one ballot is conducive to a two-party system ... Elections determined by a majority vote on one ballot literally pulverize third parties (and would do worse to fourth or fifth parties, if there were any; but none exist for this very reason). Even when a single ballot system operates with only two parties, the one that wins is favored, and the other suffers." In other words, voters tend to choose candidates who actually have a shot at winning instead of throwing their votes away on someone who will only get a small portion of the popular vote.

By contrast, "proportional representation" elections held elsewhere in the world allow for more than one candidate to be chosen from each district, or for the selection of at-large candidates. For example, if the Republican candidates win 35 percent of the vote, they would control 35 percent of the seats in the delegation; if Democrats won 40 percent, they would represent 40 percent of the delegation; and if a third party such as the Libertarians or Greens won 10 percent of the vote, they would get to hold one in 10 seats.

"The basic principles underlying proportional representation elections are that all voters deserve representation and that all political groups in society deserve to be represented in our legislatures in proportion to their strength in the electorate. In other words, everyone should have the right to fair representation," the advocacy group FairVote states.

3. It's Tough for Third Parties to Get on the Ballot

Third-party candidates have to clear greater hurdles to get on the ballot in many states, and it's difficult to raise money and organize a campaign when you're busy gathering tens of thousands of signatures. Many states have closed primaries instead of open primaries, meaning only registered Republicans and Democrats can nominate candidates for the general election. That leaves third-party candidates at a significant disadvantage. Third party candidates have less time to file paperwork and must collect a greater number of signatures than do major party candidates in some states.

4. There Are Just Too Many Third Party Candidates

There are third parties out there. And fourth parties. And fifth parties. There are, in fact, hundreds of small, obscure political parties and candidates who appear on ballots across the union in their names. But they represent a broad spectrum of political beliefs outside of the mainstream, and placing them all in a big tent would be impossible.

In the 2016 presidential election alone, voters had dozens of third-party candidates to choose from if they were dissatisfied with Republican Donald Trump and Democrat Hillary Clinton. They could have voted instead for libertarian Gary Johnson; Jill Stein of the Green Party; Darrell Castle of the Constitution Party; or Better for America's Evan McMullin. There were socialist candidates, pro-marijuana candidates, prohibition candidates, reform candidates. The list goes on. But these obscure candidates suffer from a lack of consensus, no common ideological thread running through all of them. Simply put, they're too splintered and disorganized to be credible alternatives to the major-party candidates.

Though the Democratic and Republican Parties Have Changed over Time, Their DNA Remains the Same

Dan McLaughlin

Dan McLaughlin is a senior writer for the National Review Online. He was formerly a securities and commercial litigation attorney, and his writings on politics, baseball, and law have appeared in numerous publications.

Is the Republican party dead? Has it changed irrevocably, for better or for worse, into something completely unrecognizable? Is it destined to defeat at the hands of a permanent Democratic majority? Michael Barone is here to tell you that we've heard this all before, and we should not be so hasty in projecting present trends to continue indefinitely. The seesaw rivalry of our two-party system probably isn't going away. Observers half a century from now will probably still see Republican and Democratic parties that bear many of the same characteristics that have defined each party since the middle of the 19th century.

In *How America's Political Parties Change (and How They Don't)*, a slim 118-page volume adapted from a series of lectures, Barone draws on his decades of analysis of the American political scene, his nearly bottomless well of granular knowledge of American political geography, and the more detailed analyses laid out in his multiple previous books. The result is a long-term narrative portrait of our two major parties, now both over 150 years old. The Democrats and the Republicans are, in Barone's estimation, respectively the oldest and third-oldest political parties in the world (assuming you credit his tracing of the birth of the Democrats to their 1832 convention and the birth of the British Conservative party to the 1846 rebellion against the repeal of the Corn Laws).

In Barone's telling, "America's two political parties have maintained, over their astonishingly long lifespans, their basic character, their political DNA." As he defines the central divide:

The Republican Party has always been formed around a core of people who are considered, by themselves and others, to be typical Americans, although they are never by themselves a majority: northern Protestants in the nineteenth century, married white people in the twenty-first. The Democratic Party has always been a combination, a coalition, of people who are not thought of, by themselves or others, as typical Americans, but who together often form a majority: Southern slaveholders and big-city Catholics in the nineteenth century, churchgoing and urban blacks and affluent urban and suburban liberals in the twenty-first.

The result is that Republicans, having more in common with each other, have a more cohesive identity but face a persistent struggle to broaden their appeal, while Democratic coalitions tend to be more unstable. Republican coalitions, during any period of the party's success, have always included some groups that were plainly outsiders: black freedmen in the 1870s, Mormons in the Progressive era, Cuban refugees in the 1980s. Democratic fissures, of course, have often included fights over race, but Barone also notes the party's historical divisions over foreign wars, Prohibition, labor unions, and big government.

Shifts in demographics, changes in the issue environment, and major events (wars, depressions) have forced each party to adapt and adapt again to hold coalitions together when in power and claw their way back to equilibrium when out of it. One product of these continual adaptations, reinforced by winner-take-all elections, is that American third parties only rarely break through at any level and are never able to establish themselves as long-term viable alternatives. Barone notes the rise to power of the Labour party in Britain, and other socialist-leaning workers' parties across the Western world, in the early decades of the 20th century, but in the US, even the shattering impact of the Great Depression only increased the Socialist party's vote from 0.7 percent in 1928 to 2.2 percent in 1932.

Looking at politics persistently from the bottom-up perspective of the voters, Barone gives relatively short shrift to ideology, as opposed to broad tendencies. He notes, as one example of adaptation, that the Republicans were the national-oriented party of a more active federal government from the 1850s into the 20th century but have shifted to the party we know today, a supporter of states' rights and an opponent of federal overreach. But there is more ideological continuity than change in Republican history; what looks like a shift is more a reflection of the Democrats' veering wildly from the Jacksonian extreme of localism and strict limitation of federal power to the modern Wilsonian administrative and judicial Leviathan. Few even among today's most conservative Republicans actually oppose many of the federal powers championed and exercised by the party of Lincoln and Grant. The party's Lockean core ideology, built around economic self-reliance and the right of every man to keep the fruits of what he earns, runs through every generation of Republican rhetoric, agendas, and platforms. But so does a persistent tendency toward American nationalism and Christian moralism.

In narrating the long realignment of the two parties into more ideologically sorted parties of conservatives and liberals—a realignment that, he notes, was long wished for by political scientists and reformers, and horrifies them now that it has arrived—Barone notes the role of negative partisanship. Liberal Republicans joined the Democrats as they witnessed the declining influence of people those liberals disliked: Southern segregationists, old-style urban machines, union bosses. Conservative Democrats joined the Republicans as memories of the Civil War faded, but most slowly along the line of Sherman's march. The question Barone does not attempt to forecast is whether, having sorted themselves in this way, the two parties will lose some of the fluid adaptability of their past. But his reading of the 2016 election as a Republican adaptation to the trade and foreign-policy traditions of the Midwest suggests that they have not.

Barone pushes back on two popular liberal narratives. The first is the New Deal–era view of liberal Democrats as the natural majority party. He lays out the argument that the Republican dominance of the 1920s was every bit as thoroughgoing as the Democratic dominance of the 1930s and illustrates the extent to which conservative Southern Democrats were already leaving their party's governing coalition (though not the party itself) from the late 1930s on. The resilience of the Democrats after the disasters of the 1920s and of the Republicans after the disasters of the 1930s both illustrate his thesis that the two parties are not so easily finished off.

The second is the modern progressive tendency to retell all of America's nationwide partisan history solely through the lens of race relations in the South. Barone emphasizes the long timeline of Republican inroads into the South, such as Dwight Eisenhower's drawing more popular support in the region than Goldwater, as well as the deep ancestral roots of Republican support in some parts of the upper South. While not overlooking the role of race, Barone emphasizes in particular the shift of the Democrats—the more hawkish of the two parties between 1917 and 1967—in a dovish direction on foreign policy, which helped them in the Upper Midwest (which provided most of the votes against American entry into World War I) but put the party severely out of step with the South. The primacy of foreign policy in partisan realignment goes a ways to explain why the South leaned Republican at the presidential level for decades before it shifted at the local level. He also details the long pedigree of Republican support for the rural side of intrastate rural-urban fights over drawing legislative districts in the North.

The freshest and most interesting part of the book is the concluding chapter, with its overview of the Midwest's distinctive political history, from the Northwest Ordinance to its "blue wall" support for Barack Obama and its abrupt shift in 2016 to Donald

Trump. That discussion suggests one of the major tensions within Trump's coalition, between the traditionally hawkish South and the traditionally anti-interventionist Midwest. The tension was on full display last week. On the one hand, Trump has risen in the polls in Wisconsin while he seeks to frame the House impeachment inquiry as a confrontation with the internationalist foreign-policy establishment's diplomats and national-security professionals. At the same time, the military brass is visibly uneasy at Trump's issuing pardons to soldiers accused of war crimes in Afghanistan and Iraq. Whether Trump can square the circle of presenting himself as simultaneously a take-no-prisoners hawk and an anti-"neocon" dove is exactly the sort of question that Barone asks us to consider through the lens of America's regional and partisan history.

Are Third Parties Detrimental to the Political Process?

Overview: Third-Party Candidates Face a Unique Set of Challenges

SparkNotes

SparkNotes is a company owned by Barnes & Noble that provides study guides on a number of topics related to literature, poetry, history, film, math, science, and philosophy.

Third parties face many obstacles in the United States. In all states, the Democratic and Republican candidates automatically get on the ballot, whereas third-party candidates usually have to get thousands of signatures on petitions just to be listed on the ballot. The state and federal governments, which make rules governing elections, are composed of elected Democratic and Republican officials, who have a strong incentive to protect the existing duopoly. Also, third-party candidates often face financial difficulties because a party must have received at least 5 percent of the vote in the previous election in order to qualify for federal funds.

Coke and Pepsi

The two political parties are a lot like the two giants of the cola world, Coke and Pepsi. Although each wants to win, they both recognize that it is in their mutual interest to keep a third cola from gaining significant market share. Coke and Pepsi, many people have argued, conspire to keep any competitor from gaining ground. For example, in supermarkets, cola displays at the end of the aisles are often given over to Coke for six months of the year and Pepsi for the other six. Competitors such as Royal Crown face an extremely difficult challenge. The Democrats and the Republicans function in much the same way.

SOME IMPORTANT THIRD PARTIES		
PARTY	DATES	SUCCESS(ES)
Anti-Masonic Party	1828–1832	First party to hold a convention to nominate candidates
Prohibition Party	1867–present	Has nominated a candidate for president in every election since 1872
Progressive Party	1912	Elected a number of candidates to state legislatures, Congress, and even the US Senate. Deflected enough votes from Republican William Howard Taft to hand the presidency to Democrat Woodrow Wilson in 1912.
American Independent Party	1968–present	Won electoral votes (for George Wallace)
Libertarian Party	1971–present	Some members have won local elections.
Green Party	1984–present	Some members have won local elections.

The Appeal of Third Parties

Third parties appeal to people for a number of reasons:

Ideology

People who feel strongly about a particular issue might be drawn to a third party that focuses exclusively on that issue.

Example: The Greenback Party focused on the monetary system, and the Prohibition Party sought to ban the consumption of alcohol. The Populist Party, meanwhile, grew out of the Populist movement, and the Republican Party developed primarily out of the abolitionist movement.

Dissatisfaction with the Status Quo

Some third parties form when part of a major party breaks off in protest and forms a Splinter Party.

Example: In 1912, Theodore Roosevelt led a group of dissidents out of the Republican Party to form the splinter Progressive Party.

Geographical Location

Third parties can be closely tied to a specific region, which can increase their appeal. Chicago's Harold Washington Party, for example, seeks to carry on the legacy of Harold Washington, the city's first African American mayor.

The Problem with Charismatic Leaders

Some people join third parties because of the charismatic personality of the party's candidate. If the leader leaves the party, however, the party often collapses, which is what happened to the Reform Party in the mid-1990s. Founded by Ross Perot after his first presidential bid in 1992, the Reform Party served as Perot's base for his 1996 campaign. After Perot decided not to run again, however, the Reform Party's political clout declined dramatically. In 2000, the party split in two over the candidacy of former Republican Pat Buchanan. Neither Buchanan nor his Reform Party rival gained many votes, and the party has largely disappeared from the national stage.

The Role of Third Parties

Despite their lack of success in the polls, third parties can affect American politics in a number of ways:

Introduce New Ideas

Third parties propose many government policies and practices.

Example: The Populist Party introduced ideas that influenced some economic policies of the New Deal, whereas the Anti-Masonic Party was the first party to use a convention to nominate its candidates, in the mid-nineteenth century.

Put Issues on the Agenda

Third parties can force the major parties to address potentially divisive problems.

Example: In 1992, neither Bill Clinton nor George H. W. Bush talked much about the budget deficit until independent candidate Ross Perot emphasized it in his campaign.

Spoil the Election

Third parties can cost one party an election by playing the Spoiler. If a third party draws enough votes away from a major party, it can prevent that party from winning. It is impossible to know for sure what would have happened had the third-party candidate not run, but in some cases, it seems that the third party probably cost one candidate the election.

Example: Some pundits argued that Ralph Nader's bid in the 2000 presidential election may have cost Al Gore the presidency by siphoning away votes in key states such as Florida.

Keep the Major Parties Honest

A leftist party can challenge the Democratic Party, for example, on social justice issues, whereas a conservative party can pose problems for the Republican Party. Because third-party candidates usually have little chance of winning, they can speak more frankly than their major party rivals, addressing facts and issues that the major parties would often prefer to ignore.

Third Parties Will Not Save American Politics

Nick Gillespie

Nick Gillespie is an editor-at-large at Reason, *a Libertarian magazine. He is the co-author of the book* The Declaration of Independents: How Libertarian Politics Can Fix What's Wrong with America.

G OP adviser Juleanna Glover writes in the *New York Times* that more and more "disaffected Republicans are wondering whether, if they came up with a truly great candidate, they could jump-start a new party, just as the original Republicans did in the 1850s."

If they did, they would also be delivering something that a majority of all Americans (and a super-majority of younger voters) say they want: a viable third choice in politics.

> A September Gallup poll found 61 percent of American voters support the idea of a third major political party, the highest level of support Gallup had ever recorded. Young voters seem especially eager to junk the two-party system; NBC reported in November that 71 percent of millennials want another choice.
>
> In a world in which Alabama voters elected a Democratic senator, all kinds of previously unimaginable possibilities make a new kind of sense. A third-party presidency in 2020 is no less likely today than the prospect of Donald Trump's election appeared to be two years ago.

Of course we want more choices! We can get any godd*mned coffee drink we can dream up at the s**tiest convenience store we walk into, we can choose among 50-plus gender identities on Facebook, we can instantly stream virtually any movie or TV show we hanker after. This is the golden age of personalization! Politics and the parts of our world that politics command (such as medical care and K-12 education) are the only places left

"Post-Trump, Do We Really Want a Viable Third Party? Survey Says Yes, History Says GTFO," by Nick Gillespie, Reason Foundation, January 31, 2018. Reprinted by permission.

much farther to the progressive left. Like the Roman Empire in Edward Gibbon's telling, the parties will be torn down from internal strife, not a dashing pirate swinging in to the presidential debates on a sparkly new ideological chandelier.

That's simply a reality check, though, and not cause for depression. If the Trump presidency proves anything, it's that the near-future is non-linear and anything is possible (though not predictable). The trick is for the 40 percent of us who decide every election to bend either party to our wills the way that Trump has done with Republicans. Or, as Matt Welch and I wrote in *The Declaration of Independents*, create ad hoc alliances that coalesce over specific issues and policies rather than fixating on hostile takeovers of the last remaining duopoly in American life.

The Options for Third Parties Are to Become Part of a Major Party or Resign Themselves to Stealing Away Votes

Katie McNally

Katie McNally was a university news associate at the Office of University Communications for the University of Virginia. She is now a senior communications specialist for the General Board of Higher Education and Ministry of the United Methodist Church.

It's rare that third-party outsiders can make an impact on the national political stage in the United States—but not unprecedented.

Under the rules of the Commission on Presidential Debates, presidential candidates must earn the support of at least 15 percent of voters in national polls in order to join the televised debates; recent reports suggest that Libertarian Party candidate Gary Johnson may be getting close. With less than two months to go until the first debate, he is hitting between 8 and 11 percent in various national polls—still well behind the nominees of the Democratic and Republican parties, but enough to make an impact on the outcome.

Barbara Perry, the director of presidential studies at the University of Virginia's Miller Center and co-chair of the center's Presidential Oral History program, recently discussed the impact third parties have had over the years and how they might affect the 2016 election.

"The very fact that our electoral system is a winner-take-all system discourages third parties," she said. "So almost as soon as a splinter group goes off and plans their own platform, one of the major parties, or sometimes both, try to bring those people in.

"The Third-Party Impact on American Politics," by Katie McNally, The Rector and Visitors of the University of Virginia, August 3, 2016. Reprinted by permission.

The big parties are like amoebas trying to go around the fringe groups and fold them in."

Americans have already seen this once in 2016, as the Democratic Party has stretched to include many far-left-leaning Bernie Sanders supporters. It's when the major parties are unwilling or unable to accept these differing viewpoints that third-party candidates step forward. Often their campaigns barely register on the national radar, but there are a few examples of times when they've captured just enough of the American electorate to make a difference.

Theodore Roosevelt is the most successful third-party candidate in American history. After serving as president from 1901 to 1909—first assuming office after the assassination of William McKinley and then winning the general election in 1904—Roosevelt left the Republican Party to run again in 1912 and promote a more progressive platform through his Bull Moose Party.

He earned 27 percent of the vote, effectively splitting Republican voters between himself and sitting president William Howard Taft.

"That's the most votes a third-party candidate has ever achieved," Perry said. "It was pretty amazing, but it also splintered the Republican Party, causing [Democrat] Woodrow Wilson to win the election of 1912."

The other two top third-party vote-earners of the 20th century are Robert LaFollette, who represented the Progressive Party in 1924, and Ross Perot, who ran as an independent in 1992. LaFollette took 17 percent of the popular vote, to the detriment of the Democratic Party, and Ross Perot hurt the Republicans with the 19 percent he garnered.

Perry explained the Perot is likely the best modern example of an impactful third-party candidate because his singular focus on a balanced budget forced both Republicans and Democrats to address that issue.

"When he got almost 19 percent of the vote, both Republicans and Democrats came together and balanced the budget," she said. "The success of his campaign was like a tip from the American

THIRD-PARTY CANDIDATES IN US HISTORY					
Name	Theodore Roosevelt	Robert LaFollette	Strom Thurmond	George Wallace	Ross Perot
Party	Bull Moose	Progressive	Dixiecrats	American Independent	Independent
Election Year	1912	1924	1948	1968	1992
Popular Vote	27%	17%	2%	13.5%	19%
Electoral College	88	13	39	46	0
Vote Taken From	Republicans	Democrats	Democrats	Democrats	Republicans
Election Outcome	Democratic	Republican	Democratic	Republican	Democratic

people saying, 'You better pay attention to this. If you don't pay attention, then something worse is going to happen to you in the next election.'"

While candidates like Perot may have forced changes in party agendas, it takes a major cultural and political schism for a third party to rise to the top and restructure the system. That last happened in the 1850s, when the anti-slavery movement fueled the formation of the Republican Party.

"It took the cataclysm of the Civil War and the breaking apart of the country to rejigger the parties," Perry said. "There was not an ability on the part of Democrats—who were pro-slavery, we should add—or the Whigs, who existed after the Federalists, to take this anti-slavery group under their tent. Instead, the Whig Party died and then before the Civil War, the Republican Party rises up to become the other major party alongside the Democrats."

Still, even small third-party candidates with limited success can impact the national outcome if they capture just the right percentage of votes in the right states. For this reason, Perry said disaffected Republicans who are leaning toward Gary Johnson over controversial Republican nominee Donald Trump and Bernie Sanders supporters who are leaning toward Green Party candidate Jill Stein over Democratic nominee Hillary Clinton have to ask themselves an important question: "Are you willing to accept that your third party vote may help someone you utterly disagree with?"

Perry added that Johnson and Stein still have a long way to go before they are even considered contenders for the presidential debate stage and the powerful exposure it offers, but it's not out of the realm of possibility. Stein will have to overcome poll numbers hovering below 6 percent, but most pollsters have Johnson at least halfway to the required 15 percent.

"History doesn't favor outside candidates, but common wisdom also doesn't seem to apply this election," Perry said. "If there's ever a time when third-party candidate might make it into the debates, it's this year."

More Political Parties Could Mean More Political Polarization and Greater Instability

Terrence Casey

Terrence Casey is a professor of political science and the head of the department of humanities and social sciences at the Rose-Hulman Institute of Technology in Terre Haute, Indiana. He is former executive director of the British Politics Group of the American Political Science Organization.

Americans, frustrated with the partisan machinations of the Republicans and Democrats, frequently yearn for a third party—or parties—to balance and moderate the two major ones.

On Thursday the United Kingdom will go to the polls, and all signs point to no single party winning a majority. That is, the result will be the sort of multiparty system that many American desire.

Far from moderating politics, the result has potential to make for more extreme politics and political instability.

Britain once had a stable two-party system, similar to that of the Republican/Democrat parties of the United States. In the 1950s the Conservative and Labour parties together pulled about 96 percent of the votes, and almost all of the seats in the House of Commons. The winning party would thus form a government with their leader as prime minister.

The Erosion of a Two-Party System

Over decades, that dominance has eroded such that by the 2010 general election the two main parties only polled a total of 65 percent, meaning the major parties did not have enough seats in the House of Commons to form a government. This led to a coalition government between Conservatives and the smaller

"Want More Political Parties in the US? Take a Look at Britain's Election First," by Terrence Casey, The Conversation Media Group Ltd., May 6, 2015. https://theconversation.com/want-more-political-parties-in-the-us-take-a-look-at-britains-election-first-41325. Licensed under CC BY-ND 4.0.

center-left Liberal Democrats, united in a common interest to get the budget deficit under control.

Current projections predict that Conservatives and Labour look to gain about two-thirds of the votes this time. Neither is likely to come close to a majority.

Where have their voters gone? Labour is mainly bleeding seats to a resurgent Scottish Nationalist Party (SNP). As its name implies, the SNP advocates Scottish independence. Ironically, being on the losing side on a referendum on the issue last September has energized a party that previously only won a handful of seats to the Parliament in London, as the party had positioned itself to the left of the Labour Party.

The SNP will likely take the majority of Scotland's 59 seats; some projections even have them taking them all. That's a major shift; for decades, Scotland reliably produced dozens of Labour MPs with solid majorities, akin to the typical Democratic wipeout in Massachusetts.

The Machinations and Maneuvering Needed to Create a Coalition

Prime Minister David Cameron's Conservatives face problems on two fronts. For one, their coalition partners, the Liberal Democrats, have paid the political price for the austerity policies of the past five years. Their support has slipped into single digits and the party is expected to lose half its current 57 seats.

The Conservatives are also being pressured from the right-wing UK Independence Party (UKIP), whose core mission is to make Britain independent of the European Union. UKIP's leader, Nigel Farage, with his "bloke with a pint" image and populist, anti-immigrant message, appeals to many disgruntled Conservative voters who think the current government is too moderate.

Although polling nearly 15 percent of likely voters, the vagaries of the electoral system means that the UKIP may only win a handful of seats. But the party may pull off enough Conservative voters in other constituencies to hand those seats to Labour.

What might all this mean on election day? Needing 325 seats in the House of Commons to have a majority and form a government, Labour and the Conservatives are predicted to gain only somewhere between 270 to 290 seats each, depending on swings either way.

A Labour-SNP coalition seems the most likely outcome as their combined seats may create a majority.

The Role of the Scottish Independence Party in Being a Deal Maker

Labour leader Ed Miliband and potential prime minister, however, has categorically rejected this option during the campaign. The SNP, after all, is dedicated to breaking up the United Kingdom. Even if that issue is fudged in the short term (and expect many campaign promises to fall in the sake of coalition building), the SNP is demanding the elimination of Britain's Trident submarine-based nuclear deterrent, currently stationed in Scotland, as part of any coalition deal. The SNP may be able to work out what is called a "confidence and supply" agreement with Labour, which would have the SNP supporting but not formally aligning with the government.

This arrangement would require negotiation on each individual piece of legislation. It would be difficult for a Labour government to govern effectively under such an arrangement, potentially leading to policy gridlock or governmental instability.

The Conservatives, in theory, could patch together a coalition with the LibDems, UKIP, and perhaps even the small Ulster Unionist Party. However, even with the support of these parties, Conservatives might not get a majority. Even if a coalition does emerge, relying on UKIP to govern may come at a high price, pushing the Conservatives toward an even harder line in regards to the European Union, perhaps even exiting this governing body.

In short, the rise of smaller parties, far from moderating the positions of the main parties, may push them to more extreme policies—such as abandoning Britain's nuclear deterrent or leaving the EU.

Moreover, no matter what the specifics of the arrangement, there is potential that the next British government may be hamstrung from the start due to promises made in the scramble to build a coalition and a weak and unstable majority.

Before wishing multiparty governance on the United States, we should all take a good, hard look at how this could play out in Britain first. The results may not be so pretty.

To Dismiss Third Parties Is to Ignore Significant Issues in the Two Major Parties

Fran Shor

Fran Shor is a professor emeritus of history at Wayne State University. He has written four books and is a longtime peace and justice activist.

Ralph Nader's run in the 2000 Presidential race has become for many liberals and progressives the quintessential representation of the third party "spoiler." Even invoking Nader's name in these circles induces an anger bordering on apoplexy. Without any sense of historical or political context, the Nader campaign of that year has been reduced to a hysterical and one-dimensional admonition against considering a third party presidential candidate, especially now for the 2016 Presidential election.

Before conjuring up the mythologized and reviled Nader, it behooves anyone with an ounce of critical reflection to reconstruct what led up to Nader's presidential campaign. The Clinton presidency was replete with policies that led to economic and social injustice, neoliberal globalization, and global humanitarian travesties. As Michelle Alexander and others have documented, Clinton's support for the Omnibus Crime Bill of 1994 with mandatory sentencing and expansion of the drug war and death penalties led to mass incarceration on an enormous racialized scale. Added to this was Clinton's so-called "welfare reform," which actually increased the number of women and children in poverty. Clinton's corporate agenda included deregulation of Wall Street, ending Glass-Steagall protections and leading to bank mergers and financial speculation. The promotion and passage of NAFTA only furthered job-killing corporate globalization. Finally, Clinton expanded NATO, intervened militarily in the Balkans, and created additional punitive sanctions on Iraq, the latter leading to

"It's Time to Put Ralph Nader's Role in the 2000 Election into Historical Perspective," by Fran Shor, The History News Network, August 2, 2016. Reprinted by permission.

an estimated death toll of 500,000 Iraqi children (justified by his Secretary of State, Madeline Albright).

It was revulsion with these policies, and Gore's obvious fealty to them, that led to Nader's campaign in the 2000 Presidential election. In addition, the dramatic protests in Seattle over the WTO meeting at the end of November in 1999 provided an energized base for the struggles against corporate globalization. Nader's Green Party campaign entailed ending the drug war, embracing workers' rights and fair trade, promoting free education and universal health care, and overturning corporate control of the political process. If this sounds familiar, it is very similar to the issues that Sanders ran on. However, where Sanders got around 13 million votes in the Democratic primaries, Nader's vote total in the 2000 presidential election fell short of 3 million. Moreover, it failed to gain the 5% minimum that would have guaranteed public funds for the next Green Party run in 2004.

Of course, it was Nader's near 100,000 votes in Florida that many believe cost Gore the state and, as a consequence, the electoral victory. The reality is much more complex than the simple-minded and malicious accusation that Nader cost Gore the presidency. For starters, Florida, under a Republican Secretary of State, unfairly expelled tens of thousands of its citizens, most of whom were African-American, from the voting rolls. In addition, because of the lack of standardized and comprehensible voting procedures, numerous counties had confusing ballots that contained "double bubbles," butterfly spacing, and faulty punch cards. This led to myriad voting problems, including Palm Beach votes intended for Gore that went to Pat Buchanan. Had the Gore campaign requested a recount across the state, it was clear that he would have erased by a large amount the 537 vote difference between him and Bush.

Instead of a fair and full recount of the Florida vote, the Republican Party sent in its operatives to disrupt that recount in key Democratic counties. More to the point, the partisan US Supreme Court ruled in a highly controversial and irregular 5-4 decision that the recount should not go forward. Thus, it was the Supreme

Court with relatives of Justices Scalia and Thomas working for the Bush campaign that handed the presidential election to their Republican ally.

It should also be remembered that thousands were mobilized around the country by the NAACP and other organizations to protest the shenanigans in Florida. Many of us joined these protests as soon as Florida's irregularities were known right up to the day of George W. Bush's inauguration. That millions more were not involved in stopping this political travesty is an indictment of those very liberals and progressives who now pontificate about the lesson of Nader's 2000 presidential race. People in other countries who have contended with flawed elections have managed to prevent illegimate governments from taking power. Apparently, the "limousine liberals" (as Thomas Frank labels them) and their fellow-travelers here in the US have an aversion to going out into the streets to stop what was a coup enabled by the US Supreme Court.

It is also an indictment of the political class that the arcane Electoral College has not been eliminated and significant electoral reform has not been legislated. Sixteen years later, after Gore won the popular vote by over 500,000, we are still worried about electoral swing states. Furthermore, excluding citizens from the franchise itself, like the millions of ex-felons (including what is estimated to be almost 30% of African-American men in Florida), or from voting because of ID laws that discriminate against people of color, the poor, and students calls into serious question how representative this so-called democracy is. While some cities have enacted ranked-choice voting, called IRV, and Maine will vote on establishing this state-wide in 2016, we are locked into an electoral system that makes it nearly impossible for third parties not to be cast as "spoilers."

Now we confront another presidential election, one in which the two candidates of the duopoly represent the 1%, guarantee the continuing oligarchic control of the federal government. Nonetheless, we do have a choice, but we need to recognize what might be the implications of the recent past, including the 2000 presidential election, for the present and future.

We also have to consider why we have arrived at this present political juncture. The fallout from the economic crisis of 2008 and the bailout supported by Republicans and Democrats has only increased the disenchantment with the political establishment, helping fuel the Trump and Sanders campaigns. While Trump triumphed by media enabling and racial resentment, the Sanders bid, undermined by DNC duplicity and electoral manipulation, refused to seize the historic moment and break with the Democratic Party.

Although Jill Stein of the Green Party made a bold, and to some in the Green Party controversial, offer to Sanders to be at the head of her ticket, she will instead run on a platform that improves on many of the issues advocated by Sanders, such as free college education, universal health care, ending the drug war, and enacting environmental legislation that rejects fossil fuels in favor of renewables. Moreover, Stein's Green Party positions on war and peace matters are much more advanced than Sanders from cutting the Pentagon budget by 50% to ending all of the interventions around the globe that Obama and Clinton, as Secretary of State, have promoted. For this reason alone, Stein offers a real alternative to US imperial policies that have devastated so many lives around the globe.

Stein has already begun to attract many of the disillusioned Sanderistas motivated by economic, social, racial, environmental, and global justice. Nonetheless, to capture more of those disgusted with the Trump/Clinton offering, she might want to consider actually discussing what the very real differences are between Trump and his followers and Clinton with hers. This includes denouncing the racial demagoguery of Trump and acknowledging that many people of color are part of the base of the Democratic Party. With many of the Black Lives Matter activists opting out of the presidential race and concentrating on local races for district attorneys, this may require some alliances with progressive Democrats at a local level.

Finally, whether to adopt a "safe state" or "swing state" strategy will necessitate a serious debate among Green Party members and supporters. There are those within the Green Party who believe Nader made a mistake of contesting Florida and a few other swing states in the 2000 presidential election and not concentrating on building up the vote totals in safe states like New York and California. Nonetheless, whatever the decision by Jill Stein and the Green Party concerning electoral strategy, it cannot afford merely to rely on the disgust with establishment politics to attract voters. While combating the delusion that blames Nader for Bush's election in 2000, she and the party cannot succumb to its own delusions about what can be achieved within the rigged electoral system.

Voters Often Have More in Common with Third-Party Candidates

Dominic Dezzutti

Dominic Dezzutti is the producer of the "Colorado Decides" debate series, a co-production of CBS Denver and Colorado Public Television. He is the station manager at Colorado Public Television CPT12.

Tonight, CBS 4 and Colorado Public Television kicks off our fifth election season of Colorado Decides, our election debate series. Our series this season begins with two third party candidate forums, featuring two alternate party candidates running in four different Congressional races. The episodes run on Channel 12 at 9:00pm and 9:30pm if you are interested in checking it out.

Now, you might be wondering why you should be interested in watching a forum with third party candidates. It's not likely that any of these candidates will win, so why should you spend time learning about their stance on the issues?

Although I am biased, since I am the one who hosted the forum, I think watching third party candidates talk about their stance on the issues is a valuable use of your time.

First of all, third party candidates often hold stances that are closer to the average Colorado voter than most Republican and Democratic candidates. Few third party candidates are beholden to big funders or party leaders. Frankly, many third party candidates are the kind of politicians that many of us would find appealing.

Secondly, third party candidates can be an important reminder of how our democracy is supposed to work. When this country's forefathers crafted our system of government, they envisioned citizens serving their country for a short time and then returning to their communities. The last thing they imagined would be career politicians.

"Why Third Parties Matter," by Dominic Dezzutti, CBS Broadcasting Inc., September 20, 2012. Reprinted by permission.

Third party candidates are rarely millionaires, and usually trying to run for office while still working an honest day job. They are truly examples of citizen politicians.

Third, alternate party candidates are the answer to the question many voters ask themselves in frustration every election cycle when they wonder is there any other option than simply the two major candidates in a race.

So if third party candidates have all of these positive aspects, why do we not hear about them more and why aren't they able to compete?

I don't believe in conspiracies, but in this particular case, there are direct forces working against third party candidates. Many of the rules that apply to elections and candidates are based on a two party system because they are designed by the two parties who wish to stay in power.

Another key reason we don't see third party victories very often is that most fundraising for candidates is based on desire for influence. Even if a Libertarian or a Green Party member wins a race, without a majority, they can't guarantee much influence. Without that guarantee, fundraising is impossible.

With a system working against them, and fundraising impossible, it's easier to see why we don't see more third party candidates succeed.

But at some point, our country will see third parties succeed. Sadly, it will take our current parties to hit rock bottom first. As bad as it may seem sometimes, we're nowhere near rock bottom. But at some point, we will be there.

When we hit rock bottom, it will be a dark day, but hopefully the light at the end of the tunnel will be a system that is much closer to how our government was founded, a system where alternate parties are able to see more success. It's the government our forefathers envisioned, and hopefully we can get there again.

Third Parties Have Played an Important Role in Bringing About Political Change

Robert Longley

Robert Longley is a US government and history expert with more than thirty years of experience in municipal government and urban planning.

While their candidates for President of the United States and Congress have little chance of being elected, America's third political parties have historically played a major role in bringing about sweeping social, cultural, and political reform.

Women's Right to Vote

Both the Prohibition and Socialist Parties promoted the women's suffrage movement during the late 1800s. By 1916, both Republicans and Democrats supported it and by 1920, the 19th Amendment giving women the right to vote had been ratified.

Child Labor Laws

The Socialist Party first advocated laws establishing minimum ages and limiting hours of work for American children in 1904. The Keating-Owen Act established such laws in 1916.

Immigration Restrictions

The Immigration Act of 1924 came about as a result of support by the Populist Party starting as early as the early 1890s.

Reduction of Working Hours

You can thank the Populist and Socialist Parties for the 40-hour work week. Their support for reduced working hours during the 1890s led to the Fair Labor Standards Act of 1938.

"The Important Role of US Third Parties," by Robert Longley, Dotdash Publishing Family, July 2, 2019. Reprinted by permission.

Income Tax

In the 1890s, the Populist and Socialist Parties supported a "progressive" tax system that would base a person's tax liability on their amount of income. The idea led to the ratification of the 16th Amendment in 1913.

Social Security

The Socialist Party also supported a fund to provide temporary compensation for the unemployed in the late 1920s. The idea led to the creation of laws establishing unemployment insurance and the Social Security Act of 1935.

"Tough on Crime"

In 1968, the American Independent Party and its presidential candidate George Wallace advocated "getting tough on crime." The Republican Party adopted the idea in its platform and the Omnibus Crime Control and Safe Streets Act of 1968 was the result. (George Wallace won 46 electoral votes in the 1968 election. This was the highest number of electoral votes collected by a third party candidate since Teddy Roosevelt, running for the Progressive Party in 1912, won a total of 88 votes.)

America's First Political Parties

The Founding Fathers wanted the American federal government and its inevitable politics to remain non-partisan. As a result, the US Constitution makes no mention whatsoever of political parties.

In Federalist Papers No. 9 and No. 10, Alexander Hamilton and James Madison respectively refer to the dangers of political factions they had observed in the British government. America's first president, George Washington, never joined a political party and warned against the stagnation and conflict they can cause in his Farewell Address.

> However [political parties] may now and then answer popular ends, they are likely in the course of time and things, to

become potent engines, by which cunning, ambitious, and unprincipled men will be enabled to subvert the power of the people and to usurp for themselves the reins of government, destroying afterwards the very engines which have lifted them to unjust dominion.

— George Washington, Farewell Address,
September 17, 1796

However, it was Washington's own closest advisers who spawned the American political party system. Hamilton and Madison, despite writing against political factions in the Federalist Papers, became the core leaders of the first two functional opposing political parties.

Hamilton emerged as the leader of the Federalists, who favored a strong central government, while Madison and Thomas Jefferson led the Anti-Federalists, who stood for a smaller, less-powerful central government. It was the early battles between the Federalists and Anti-Federalists that spawned the environment of partisanship that now dominates all levels of American government.

Leading Modern Third Parties

While the following is far from all of the recognized third parties in American politics, the Libertarian, Reform, Green, and Constitution Parties are usually the most active in presidential elections.

Libertarian Party

Founded in 1971, the Libertarian party is the third largest political party in America. Over the years, Libertarian Party candidates have been elected to many state and local offices.

Libertarians believe the federal government should play a minimal role in the day-to-day affairs of the people. They believe that the only appropriate role of government is to protect the citizens from acts of physical force or fraud. A libertarian-style government would, therefore, limit itself to a police, court, prison system and military. Members support the free market economy and are dedicated to the protection of civil liberties and individual freedom.

Reform Party

In 1992, Texan H. Ross Perot spent over $60 million of his own money to run for president as an independent. Perot's national organization, known as "United We Stand America" succeeded in getting Perot on the ballot in all 50 states. Perot won 19 percent of the vote in November, the best result for a third party candidate in 80 years. Following the 1992 election, Perot and "United We Stand America" organized into the Reform Party. Perot again ran for president as the Reform Party candidate in 1996 winning 8.5 percent of the vote.

As its name implies, Reform Party members are dedicated to reforming the American political system. They support candidates they feel will "re-establish trust" in government by displaying high ethical standards coupled with fiscal responsibility and accountability.

Green Party

The American Green Party's platform is based on the following 10 Key Values:

- Ecological wisdom
- Community-based economics
- Grassroots democracy
- Decentralization
- Gender equality
- Personal and social responsibility
- Respect for diversity
- Nonviolence
- Global responsibility

"Greens seek to restore balance through recognizing that our planet and all of life are unique aspects of an integrated whole, and also through affirming the significant inherent values and contribution of each part of that whole." The Green Party–Hawaii

Constitution Party

In 1992, American Taxpayer Party presidential candidate Howard Phillips appeared on the ballot in 21 states. Mr. Phillips again ran in 1996, achieving ballot access in 39 states. At its national convention in 1999, the party officially changed its name to the "Constitution Party" and again chose Howard Phillips as its presidential candidate for 2000.

The Constitution Party favors a government based on a strict interpretation of the US Constitution and the principals expressed in it by the Founding Fathers. They support a government limited in scope, structure, and power of regulation over the people. Under this goal, the Constitution Party favors a return of most governmental powers to the states, communities and the people.

CHAPTER 3

Can Third Parties Represent American Values?

Overview: Individual Differences in Third-Party Candidates and Structural Factors Impact Their Success in Presidential Races

Daniel Bush

Daniel Bush is a senior political reporter for PBS NewsHour. *He is based in Washington, DC.*

If given the chance, Gary Johnson and Jill Stein would have used the upcoming debates to remind voters that Donald Trump and Hillary Clinton won't be the only presidential candidates on the ballot come November.

But Johnson, a former governor of New Mexico and the Libertarian Party nominee, and Stein, who is running on the Green Party ticket, failed to qualify for the presidential debates, which begin next week at Hofstra University on Long Island.

The news, which was announced last week, was not a surprise. Neither third-party candidate came close to meeting the polling threshold of 15 percent to participate in the debates.

Nevertheless, in an election driven by voter frustration with the political establishment, Johnson and Stein could still do reasonably well in November—and potentially play a spoiler role in the final outcome, if the third-party candidates hurt Trump or Clinton in critical swing states. The prospect of a solid showing this year highlights one of the most confounding aspects of American politics: the electorate's inconsistent, back-and-forth appetite for third-party candidates.

When it comes to non-major-party candidates, differences in political talent and experience help explain why some perform better than others.

But in interviews, political scientists, strategists and current and former third-party nominees all agreed that structural

"What Would It Take for a Third-Party Candidate to Make It to the White House?" by Daniel Bush, PBS NewsHour Online, September 25, 2016. Reprinted by permission.

factors—such as access to campaign cash and media exposure—determine whether third party candidates break into the national consciousness or not.

"It has less to do with the characteristics of the individual candidate, and more to do with how well things are going in the country," said Robert Shapiro, a political scientist at Columbia University. "What it really comes down to is the level of dissatisfaction with government, and whether there's an open space on the ideological spectrum for a third or fourth-party candidate."

In an interview on Wednesday, Johnson argued that voters this election were seeking alternative options to avoid supporting Clinton and Trump. "In this case you've got the two most polarizing figures of all time and space that are the two major party candidate nominees," Johnson said.

Third-party candidates have been shut out of the presidency since the rise of the two-party system in the mid-1800s. The most successful third-party candidates in the past century have capitalized on political divisions within the two major parties that came about as a result of economic and cultural turmoil in the country.

Consider Theodore Roosevelt. In 1912, four years after his presidency ended, Roosevelt took advantage of a split in the Republican Party to mount an independent run on the Progressive Party ticket. Roosevelt had unusually high name recognition for a third-party candidate, but still only managed to win six states and 88 electoral college votes, finishing a distant second to Woodrow Wilson.

The next serious third-party challenger, George Wallace, built his 1968 presidential campaign around a strategy of appealing to white Southern Democrats who opposed the party's embrace of the Civil Rights movement.

Wallace, a former governor of Alabama who was best known for his support of segregation, won a total of five states and 46 electoral college votes. He is the last third-party candidate to sweep a state's electoral college votes, according to the historian

Dan Carter, who has written about Wallace and the rise of modern American conservatism.

But all of Wallace's victories took place in the Deep South, in states that Richard Nixon was likely to win in a two-way contest against Hubert Humphrey, the Democratic nominee.

Wallace seized on the racial prejudice of the era to run the most successful third-party campaign since Roosevelt's, but his divisive approach only took him so far. "His main impact was carrying states that probably would have gone for Nixon," Carter said. "In terms of the final vote, he was a regional candidate."

More than two decades later, Ross Perot turned out to be that rare third-party candidate with true national appeal.

A Texas-born billionaire with no prior political experience, Perot used his wealth to run lengthy, chart-laden campaign ads that raised his standing in the polls in the 1992 presidential election, helping him land a spot in the debates with George H.W. Bush and Bill Clinton.

"He was so weird that he captured the imagination. His tone of voice, his style, we'd never seen anything like it before," said Bill Miller, a veteran lobbyist and political observer in Texas.

Perot was a gifted performer. But he also benefited from events at the time that created a unique opportunity for a plainspoken, outsider candidate to step in and challenge the status quo. In 1992, the economy was mired in a recession; Republicans were upset with President Bush for breaking his campaign promise not to raise taxes; and many voters were eager for a change after 12 years of Republican rule in the White House.

"For a third-party person to be successful, there has to be voter anger, and the candidate has to channel that," Miller said. "And that's not easy. That's why most of them are unsuccessful."

That fall, Perot won 19 percent of the popular vote, the second-highest total for a third-party candidate in modern US history (after Roosevelt, who won 27 percent in 1912). But because Perot's supporters were evenly distributed around the country, he failed to win a single electoral college vote. He fared even worse in his second presidential campaign four years later.

The most famous American third-party presidential candidate, arguably, is Ralph Nader, whom many Democrats still blame for the outcome of the 2000 presidential race.

Running as a Green Party candidate, Nader received 2.7 percent of the popular vote, a fraction of George W. Bush and Al Gore's support. But Nader won about 97,000 votes in Florida, which Bush ultimately carried by just 537 votes after a recount battle that reached the Supreme Court.

Nader's critics have long argued that Gore would have also won the state of New Hampshire, and avoided a recount, if Nader had not been on the ballot and a majority of the state's Green Party supporters had backed the Democratic nominee.

Nader defended his 2000 campaign in an interview on Monday in New York, arguing that the race in Florida was decided by the thousands of Democratic voters who crossed party lines to support Bush.

In reflecting back on that race, and his subsequent, less-controversial White House bids in 2004 and 2008, Nader blamed the two major parties and the media for making it difficult for third-party candidates to compete in presidential elections.

"Here's the interesting thing when you don't get media," said Nader, who sat for an interview in between promotional stops for a new book, *Breaking Through Power*. "I was probably known by 80 percent of the people as a consumer advocate. And I think 80 percent of the people didn't even know I was running."

Nader cited a study in a book by the academics Stephen Farnsworth and S. Robert Lichter that found he received just three minutes of speaking time on the evening news shows of the three major broadcast networks between Labor Day and Election Day in 2000. During that same time period, ABC, NBC and CBS broadcast a combined 53 minutes of uninterrupted speech by Gore, and 42 minutes by Bush.

Farnsworth, one of the report's co-authors and a political science professor at the University of Mary Washington, confirmed the statistics in a phone interview.

"What's very clear is that reporters focus on the two major-party candidates. So if you're a third-party candidate and you don't posses the vast personal fortune of a Ross Perot, you're going to be ignored," Farnsworth said. "Presidential candidates who do not have a D or R after their name are finished before they even start."

Terry Holt, a former top Bush campaign adviser, argued that Nader wasn't a factor in the race. "There's always an undercurrent of dissatisfaction with the major party candidates," Holt said. "Al Gore had a weak spot in his base of support that he could never close."

In the interview with *PBS NewsHour*, Nader, who is 82, focused on the media's role in covering third-party presidential candidates. But he also acknowledged that he could have chosen to run more traditional campaigns that centered on a few signature issues.

"My problem is, I ran on too many issues," he said. "People would say, 'Narrow the issues.' And I would say, 'No, I don't want to. I want to make a declaration.'"

Johnson and Stein have largely followed Nader's make-a-declaration approach in 2016. It may not have gotten them into the debates, but Johnson is averaging around 8 percent in national polls, and Stein is polling around three percent. In one Quinnipiac University survey earlier this month, they polled a combined 17 percent—nearly the total Perot received on Election Day in 1992.

Johnson is drawing support from Democrats and Republicans, though some polls show that a majority of his backers are Republican, a sign that he could hurt Trump more than Clinton. In a recent CBS/NYT poll, for instance, Johnson received 13 percent support from likely voters. Among that group, 8 percent said they leaned Republican, compared to 6 percent who said they leaned Democratic.

With seven weeks left in the race, it's still too early to tell what the third-party effect will be. But if Johnson, who is polling better than Stein, maintains his current level of support, he could change the outcome in some key battleground states.

In Florida, Clinton and Trump were tied at 43.3 percent in a national average of polls taken in the first three weeks of September. Johnson averaged 6 percent, more than enough to sway the race towards one of the major party nominees. Johnson is currently polling at roughly 8 percent in Ohio, another crucial swing state that has tightened in recent weeks.

Johnson claimed that he would finish much higher if he had qualified for the debates. "Ross Perot was polling lower than I am right now when he was allowed into the debates," Johnson said in his interview with *PBS NewsHour.* "And when he was allowed into the debates at one point he was actually leading in that race."

But experts cautioned that many polls inflate the public's support for third-party candidates.

"In a poll, the voter is offered the candidates' names; this isn't the same thing as what a random voter may know," Micah Sifry, the author of *Spoiling for a Fight: Third-Party Politics in America,* wrote in an email.

He added, "While many voters may be unhappy with the choice of Trump or Clinton, not that many are aware of Johnson or Stein, because they have little money or visibility. That's why typically third-party presidential candidates always underperform their polling."

Sifry noted that Perot was the sole exception.

Robert Shapiro, the political scientist at Columbia University, said that future presidential races could feature more third-party candidates if the two major parties continue to grow further apart.

"The one thing that's been happening since the 1970s is increasing polarization and divergence between the parties," he said. "The Republican Party is becoming a consistently conservative party and the Democratic Party is becoming consistently liberal, leaving an opening in the middle."

But Shapiro said that doesn't guarantee the next generation of third-party candidates will be any more successful than the last.

"What makes it imprecise is that you don't know what would happen if [third party candidates] weren't on the ticket. Would people vote for the mainstream candidates or not vote at all?" he said. "There's no science."

The Two-Party System Is a Political Monopoly That Needs to Be Broken Up

Jim Jonas

Jim Jonas is the chief political strategist for the Serve America Movement (SAM) Party, a third party that is focused on fixing the political system by offering voters more choices. He is based in Denver, Colorado.

Facebook co-founder Chris Hughes recently made the argument in the *New York Times* for the break up of the social media giant by arguing it has become a dangerous monopoly that places too much power and influence in the hands of one company and one person (his former Harvard roommate, Mark Zuckerberg).

While the column was an interesting insight into the influential power and online stranglehold Facebook wields over social media, what struck me most was the corollary between Facebook's social media dominance and that of the anti-competitive two-party monopoly's vice grip on American politics.

Hughes may be right that it's time to break up the Facebook monopoly (though there's not an easy path to do so). And I'm quite sure it's past time to break up our country's two-party monopoly (which will also be hard—but well worth the effort).

In his column, Hughes wrote: "America was built on the idea that power should not be concentrated in any one person (or company), because we are all fallible. That's why the founders created a system of checks and balances. They didn't need to foresee the rise of Facebook to understand the threat that gargantuan companies would pose to democracy. Jefferson and Madison were voracious readers of Adam Smith, who believed that monopolies prevent the competition that spurs innovation and leads to economic growth."

"It's Time to Break Up the Two-Party Monopoly," by Jim Jonas, InsideSources, June 18, 2019. Reprinted by permission.

Clearly, we have an obligation to prevent monopolies in critical industries and the nation's resource providers.

So why aren't we more outraged by the political monopoly that utterly dominates our elections, suppresses competition and systematically stomps out common-sense electoral reforms that would pave the way for better elected leadership?

Sadly, the electorate has been largely anesthetized to political dysfunction assuming that the system we have is the best we can do. That's exactly what partisan leaders want us to believe. They have no interest nor incentive to either change the way elections work nor in actually solving the existential public policy challenges we face. In fact, major party elected leaders have significant disincentives to reaching common-ground solutions as their rabid "base" voters threaten to withhold financial support, recruit primary challengers or go on their favorite partisan TV network to clamp down on apostates who don't toe the party line.

But wait, you say, there are two parties … aren't they in competition with each other?

Not so much.

The two dominant political parties may not agree on solutions to hot-button policy disagreements. But they're in complete cahoots when it comes to blocking more competition from entering the political system. From ballot access and campaign finance restrictions to gerrymandered districts, the system is littered with anti-competitive rules that protect the two-party monopoly instead of encouraging the emergence of new voices and choices that will demand real progress on fixing problems.

And without that competition there is little incentive for the parties to change their behavior.

So until we inject more competition into the system and demand that candidates and parties actively compete for voters' support, we won't see progress on the big problems facing America—just more finger pointing and gamesmanship for partisan re-election advantage. There's no incentive to do otherwise.

So how to get more competition into the political system?

First, we need to mind shift the electorate's perception that elections should be about serving the interests of individual voters and not the political parties. That means implementing common sense reforms like nonpartisan redistricting, ballot and debate access so voters hear from more voices in elections, open primaries so all voters can participate in primary elections, ranked choice voting and other electoral advances that encourage more than just the two parties to credibly compete in general elections and much more. There are several prominent national organizations making great headway on putting game-changing electoral reforms in front of legislatures and on state ballots this year.

But electoral reforms aren't enough on their own. The system demands we build a viable national party of influence that can directly challenge the two-party monopoly and will force greater competition into the political marketplace. This new party will be driven by a fundamentally different approach to leadership based not on the one-dimensional, left-right, conservative-liberal spectrum the parties use to pigeonhole voters. Instead, this new party will focus on problem-solving leadership with accountability, transparency, accessibility, collaboration and voter engagement as its highest values.

Because here's the truth that the parties don't want voters to realize: Americans agree much more on solutions to the big problems than we disagree.

But the stale two-party monopoly won't let us get to collaborative solutions because there is no incentive for either side to collaborate or compromise.

And that's where SAM [Serve America Movement] comes in: To be that competitive incentive to demand action on the nation's pressing policy challenges.

Building a new national party of national influence isn't easy. And we'll have a lot more to share as we develop our new way of leadership and how to message it to voters. But the need to challenge the two-party monopoly has never been greater. We hope you'll join SAM in figuring out how to best break it up.

Third-Party Candidates Sometimes Receive Significant Support from Voters

Oishimaya Sen Nag

Oishimaya Sen Nag holds a PhD and is a full-time freelance writer and editor based in Kolkata, India.

United States politics is often characterized as a "two-party" system. For much of its history, these two dominant parties have been the Republican and Democratic party, with the Whigs, Federalists, and Democratic-Republicans dominating portions of its earlier years. Nonetheless, third-party and Independent candidates have also at times fared well as well. This is evidenced by the ten men listed below, who each snagged significant numbers of popular votes, and some from the Electoral College as well, in their respective bids for the White House and US Presidency.

10. William Wirt, Anti-Masonic, 1832 (7 Electoral Votes)

In the 1820s, an Anti-Masonic Movement flourished in the United States, fueled by public suspicion in regards to the existence of a secret and powerful fraternal order, namely the Free Masons. The movement was triggered with the mysterious disappearance of William Morgan, who was believed to have been murdered by the Masons for breaking his vow of secrecy and preparing a book. The book supposedly revealed many of the close-kept secrets of the Masonic order. During this time, the Anti-Masonic Party became an influential political party, and were the first American third party to hold a national nominating convention. There, William Wirt was nominated as the Anti-Masonic Presidential candidate for the 1932 US Presidential Election. Though Wirt only won

Sen Nag, Oishimaya. "Most Successful Third Party US Presidential Candidates." WorldAtlas, Sept. 26, 2018, worldatlas.com/articles/most-successful-third-party-us-presidential-candidates.html. Reprinted by permission.

7 electoral votes in the state of Vermont, and his party fell into decline shortly thereafter, his minor victory is still recorded as one of the most successful US third party ventures in the history of the country's Presidential elections.

9. Millard Fillmore, American, 1856 (8 Electoral Votes)

Millard Fillmore was the 13th US President, and the one who served office between 1850 and 1853. He was also the last US President not to be affiliated with either the Democrats or the Republicans. In 1856, former President Fillmore, then affiliated with the American Party, was nominated as a Presidential candidate for the Presidential elections in 1856. The other two candidates, James Buchanan and John C. Frémont, represented the Democrats and Republicans, respectively. While slavery was an omnipotent issue discussed in the election campaigns of 1856, the American Party decided to largely ignore this issue and instead focus on anti-immigration and anti-Catholic policies. Fillmore also focused on the point that the American Party was the only "national party" in the true sense, as the Republicans were fanatically in favor of the North's interests and the Democrats leaned towards those of the South. However, in the end, Buchanan defeated both Fillmore and Frémont to become the 15th President of the United States. Only 8 electoral votes were won by Fillmore, which was still a significant number when considering the historical stance of third parties in the Presidential elections of the country.

8. John Floyd, Nullifier, 1832 (11 Electoral Votes)

The Nullifier Party, a short lived national political party based in South Carolina, was founded in 1828 by John C. Calhoun. It was so named as its members felt that constituent US states should have the right to "null and void" certain Federal legislation. This ranged from slavery laws to the imposition of tariffs and embargoes. The party campaigned for states' rights and supported the related Kentucky and Virginia Resolutions. In the 1832 US presidential elections, the Nullifier Party nominated John Floyd, an ally of Calhoun, as the Presidential candidate from the party. Though Floyd suffered defeat in the elections, he still managed to grab 11 electoral votes in the election.

7. Robert La Follette, Progressive, 1924 (13 Electoral Votes)

In the 1924 US presidential elections, Robert La Follette, a former Governor of Wisconsin (1901–1906) and a Progressive Party-nominated Presidential candidate, won almost 5 million popular votes, equating to one-sixth of the total votes cast, establishing his name in the list of America's most successful third party candidates in history. Though he won only 13 electoral votes, and carried just his own state of Wisconsin in the end, he is still remembered for his contributions in exposing some of the most glaring corruption cases of the post-World War I years in the country.

6. James Weaver, People's Party, 1892 (22 Electoral Votes)

The 1892 US Presidential elections witnessed a significant influence of the People's Party, led by James Weaver, in the poll results. Though the Presidential position was in the end won by the Democratic candidate, Grover Cleveland, against the Republican candidate, Benjamin Harrison, and the People's Party candidate, James Weaver, Weaver, with his patriarchal presence and commanding influence, still managed to secure 22 electoral votes and 1,041,028 popular votes in the election that year. Weaver and the People's Party's platform demanded free and unlimited coinage of silver. The party also supported the government ownership of the railroads. In 1896, however, the influence of the People's Party waned away as Weaver assigned the Party's presidential nomination to William J. Bryan, a progressive, former Democratic candidate. In his later years, Weaver served as a small-town Iowa mayor and local historian.

5. John Bell, Constitutional Union, 1860 (39 Electoral Votes)

The Constitutional Union Party was a US political party formed in 1859 by former Whigs and members of the Know-Nothing Party. In the 1860 Presidential elections, the party nominated John Bell for US President. The party sought to rally for support of the Union and the Constitution, and paid little attention to sectionally divisive issues such as slavery in its Presidential campaign. The ignorance of the slavery issue cut down Bell's votership bank significantly, but he still managed to win 39 electoral votes, particularly in the border states of the country who were sentimentally torn between the regional interests of the North and the South. Even though the party had collapsed by the beginning of the Civil War, Bell's candidature in the elections was able to sufficiently disperse the votes so as to allow the Republican candidate, Abraham Lincoln, to more easily come to power as the President of United States.

4. Strom Thurmond, States' Rights Dixiecrats, 1948 (39 Electoral Votes)

James Strom Thurmond was a famous American politician who served in the post of Senator from South Carolina for a period of 48 years. In 1948, he fought in the Presidential elections and, though he did not win, he was largely successful in receiving 39 Electoral votes and 2.4% of the national popular votes in the election. Thurmond was nominated as Presidential candidate by the States' Rights Democratic Party, or the "Dixiecrats," which was established after a split from the national Democrats over the issue of Federal intervention in state affairs, especially civil rights and segregation, by the then-ruling Democrats. Thurmond was, however, defeated by the incumbent Democratic President Harry S. Truman, who earned people's votes for his policies favoring the end of racial discrimination in US Army, the support of the elimination of state poll taxes, and Federal anti-lynching laws, as well as the creation of a permanent Fair Employment Practices Commission.

Thurmond served into the new millennium, having had softened, and even condemned, his former racist and segregationist stances.

3. George Wallace, American Independent, 1968 (46 Electoral Votes)

The American Independent Party was founded by George Wallace, a previous Democrat, when his racist, pro-segregation policies had been rejected by the mainstream Democrats. In the 1968 US Presidential elections, Wallace represented the American Independent Party as their Presidential candidate. Wallace was a realist who knew their were slim chances of winning the polls, but he hoped to receive enough Electoral votes to act as a "power broker" in the House of Representatives to decide the election. His campaign, which supported racial segregation, was popular with rural white southerners and blue-collar union workers throughout much of the country, and he managed to capture 13.53% of the popular vote and 46 Electoral votes in the elections. However, Wallace was unsuccessful in capturing enough votes to throw the election to the House and exert his influence on the selection of the President. Like Thurmond, Wallace also later significantly changed his views on race relations, especially after devoting himself as an Evangelical Christian.

2. John Breckinridge, Constitutional Democrat, 1860 (72 Electoral Votes)

John Breckinridge began his political career by winning a seat in the Kentucky House of Representatives in 1849. His political career soared to its highest point ever when he was elected as the 14th Vice President of the US in 1856, becoming the youngest vice president in the country's history. In 1860, he ran for President himself in the US Presidential elections, representing a Southern fraction of the Democratic Party. His campaigns were in favor of slavery, and he demanded Federal intervention to protect slaveholders in their own territories. His campaigns, however, did not win him much popularity, and he lost the election to the other candidates, namely Republican Lincoln and Democrat Douglas. Breckinridge still earned 72 electoral votes and 848,019 popular votes, accounting for 18.1% of the entire voter pool. His achievements in this election, though not sufficient to let him win, recorded his name in the history of the United States as the second most successful third party Presidential candidate.

1. Teddy Roosevelt, Progressive, 1912 (88 Electoral Votes)

In the 1912 US Presidential elections, former President Teddy Roosevelt emerged as the most successful third party presidential candidate in the history of the country when he bagged 88 Electoral votes and 27% of the popular vote in the election on behalf of the Progressive Party of the United States. The party was formed by Roosevelt himself when he failed to receive the nomination from the Republican Party in the 1912 Elections. However, Roosevelt lost, and the election was won by the Democratic Party's nominee, Woodrow Wilson, who went on to become the 28th President of the United States. The 1912 Presidential elections were unique in the fact that this was the last election where a candidate who was neither Republican nor Democrat came second in the election. This occurred as Teddy Roosevelt defeated Republican William Howard Taft and Socialist Eugene Debs.

Democratic Socialism Resonates with Young Voters

Lauren Gambino

Lauren Gambino is a senior political correspondent for the Guardian US. She is based in Washington, DC.

The last time the nation's largest socialist organization came together for its biennial conference, congresswoman Alexandria Ocasio-Cortez was serving tacos and cocktails at a bar in Manhattan.

Two years later, the Democratic Socialists of America have doubled in size and the young, Latina, democratic socialist from the Bronx who unseated a 10-term veteran to win her New York congressional seat has become a political force so visible she is known simply by her initials, AOC.

Nearly 100 democratic socialists now hold elected office across the country, from school boards to state legislatures and Congress, where Ocasio-Cortez and the Michigan congresswoman Rashida Tlaib have become avatars of an emboldened leftwing insurgency. The Vermont senator Bernie Sanders, whose popularity has helped soften public perception of socialism though he is not directly involved with DSA, is a top-tier candidate for the 2020 Democratic nomination while Donald Trump is running for re-election on campaign slogans portraying socialism as a direct threat to America.

The DSA, founded in 1982, has never had more of a national presence in US politics. Now, as socialism moves from the margins of American political life to the center of presidential politics, the movement faces a new and welcome challenge: where to go from here?

"'We're Here to Win': US Democratic Socialists Move to Center Stage," by Lauren Gambino, Guardian News & Media Limited, August 6, 2019. Reprinted by permission.

"We're not interested in losing and we're not interested in performing our politics," Maria Svart, DSA's national director told the more than 1,000 democratic socialists who gathered in Atlanta last week for DSA's largest-ever conference. "We're here to win. And at a grand scale we want to transform society."

Over the course of four days, in a conference room at the Westin Peachtree Plaza, a unionized hotel in downtown Atlanta, members, ecstatic over their growing ranks and electoral victories, envisioned a society untethered from traditional capitalism. But more immediately, they debated strategy and structure. The divisions over how DSA can best capitalize on a surge of interest echoed the central debate over the future of the Democratic party pitting pragmatism against ideological purity.

"Right now so much is possible and it's incredibly exciting," said David Duhalde, the former deputy director of DSA who recently worked for the Sanders-aligned, Our Revolution. "But that also begets many, many more debates and questions about how we move forward and that is a great problem to have."

In a series of votes, members approved measures to prioritize electing democratic socialists at every level of government and to grow membership, currently at 56,000, to 100,000 while rejecting a proposal to adopt national political "litmus tests" for candidates. They will continue to run primary challenges against centrist Democrats and to organize low-income, working people, including in communities that voted for Trump.

Amid much debate, DSA, which enthusiastically backed Sanders earlier this year, passed a resolution titled "In the event of a Sanders loss," stipulating that the group would not formally endorse another Democratic presidential nominee if the Vermont senator does not win the primary.

Members also voted to support the Green New Deal, universal childcare, the decriminalization of sex work and "open borders"—a radical idea that goes far beyond what any Democratic presidential candidate would endorse. They also reaffirmed their support for the controversial Boycott, Divestment, Sanctions movement to protest against Israel's treatment of Palestine and narrowly voted to establish an "anti-fascist working group".

But even for veterans, the hours-long debate—frequently interrupted by arcane procedural inquiries strictly governed by Robert's Rules of Order—was a slog. Efforts to keep the discussion "comradely" by stifling side chatter and using gender-neutral terms drew snickers from conservative media.

At one point during a back and forth over whether to expand the organization's national staff, an irritated delegate stepped to the microphone to raise a point of order.

"Can we *please* use 'comrade' as an honorific instead of 'sir' or 'madam'?" the delegate asked tersely. The chair quickly apologized and thanked the "comrade" for raising the point.

DSA's numbers are relatively small, but its outsized impact on the conversation has caused a political headache for mainstream Democrats who reject any association with socialism.

During the presidential debate in Detroit, centrist John Hickenlooper, the former governor of Colorado, said Sanders' policies, including Medicare for All and a Green New Deal would be a "disaster at the ballot box."

"You might as well FedEx the election to Donald Trump," he said.

Not far from the Westin, where DSA members made plans to grow their ranks, Vice-President Mike Pence implored conservative youth to resist the "siren song of socialism."

"It's not going to be enough just to win the next election," he said at the Resurgent Gathering in Atlanta on Friday. "We got to win the next generation. We got to go tell the story to younger Americans about the truth—the truth about socialist policies."

But a May Gallup poll found an increasing number of Americans—four in 10—believe some form of socialism would be good for the country, though more than half still disagree.

At rallies and on social media, Trump has sought to portray all his Democrat adversaries as socialists intent on bringing "unAmerican," European-style welfare programs across the

Atlantic. These ideological attacks, which he has paired with racist and anti-immigrant rhetoric, are part of a political strategy to galvanize his core followers.

"Trump is attacking us because the socialist movement offers an alternative vision to what he is offering, which is essentially neo-fascism," said Svart, DSA's national director. "He is threatened by us. And so are the Wall Street Democrats."

She continued: "What we're saying as democratic socialists is that none of it has to be this way."

Most new DSA members are young, millennials who came of age during the global financial crisis, like Rachel Kahn. But the group's numbers didn't start to rise until Sanders ran for president in 2016.

"He was the person who made me realize that I'm a socialist," Kahn, 29, said on a break during the conference.

Polling suggest that young people are increasingly disillusioned by capitalism and more open to socialism than previous generations. At the same time, young people are more likely to associate socialism with the Scandinavian-style social welfare state than with Soviet communism.

Though it was her first time attending a DSA conference since she joined a local Atlanta chapter, Kahn spoke passionately on several resolutions, particularly those she thought might affect candidates in the south.

On a question about litmus tests, she said forcing southern candidates to identify as "democratic socialists" would be a "death sentence." The resolution failed.

"People here are so institutionally primed to have a visceral, negative reaction to socialism," she said. "If we want to win here," she said afterward, "that might require molding ourselves to our environment a little bit and leading with our values instead."

khalid kamau, a member of the city council in South Fulton, Georgia, and first #BlackLivesMatter organizer elected to public office, told the conference: "We have to understand that us fringe people are future thinkers."

At a press conference later that weekend, he joined nearly two dozen locally elected democratic socialists, including from traditionally Republican areas. The slate included Ruth Buffalo, a Native American representative in North Dakota who ousted the sponsor of the state's ID law, Mik Pappas, a district judge in Pennsylvania who has sought to end cash bail in his court, and a contingent of the six democratic socialists recently elected to Chicago's 50-member city council.

"It's a recognition that capitalism has failed us," Gabriel Acevero, who was elected to the Maryland state house of delegates in 2018, said of their growing ranks in elected office. "Capitalism has failed working people. Capitalism has failed oppressed people and capitalism has failed our planet. And I think more and more people are coming to that realization."

Near the end of a long day of debate, cheers rang out in the conference room. Sean Parker, a democratic socialist in Nashville, had just won a seat on the city council.

Libertarianism Has Gained Traction with Mainstream Conservatives

Gene H. Bell-Villada

Gene H. Bell-Villada is a professor of Romance languages at Williams College. He has authored and edited ten books, including On Nabokov, Ayn Rand and the Libertarian Mind: What the Russian-American Odd Pair Can Tell Us about Some Values, Myths and Manias Widely Held Most Dear.

Ayn Rand (1904–82) has arisen from the dead. Over the last decade the pop philosopher and propaganda fictionist extraordinaire has moved steadily from the cultish margins to the mainstream of US conservatism.

Her ghost may even haunt the current presidential race with the candidacy of Republican Senator Rand Paul, a libertarian darling who received a set of Ayn Rand books for his 17th birthday.

In her bestselling books and essays, Rand frankly celebrated selfishness and greed—and the underside of this celebration is a scorn toward and demonization of any simple caring about other human beings. Such a stance has become a hidden, yet driving force behind such loaded catchphrases as "spending cuts" and, more grandiosely, "limited government."

In a larger sense, though, Rand had never died. Sales of her books remained steadily in the six figures in the years following her demise, their underground influence an unacknowledged-if-discomforting fact of American life. A couple of reader surveys carried out in the 1990s by Book-of-the-Month Club and the Library of Congress, and by the Modern Library imprint, showed Rand's *Atlas Shrugged* and *Fountainhead* near the top of the polling results, according to author Brian Doherty. And, in the wake of the 2008 financial meltdown, sales of her works tripled.

Randianism, what she called Objectivism, now exists as a mass phenomenon, a grass-roots presence, a kind of folklore. "Who Is John Galt?", her recurring slogan from *Atlas Shrugged*, can be seen on placards at Tea Party rallies, on leaflets casually affixed to telephone poles or on the shopping bags of Lululemon Athletics, the Canadian sports apparel company. The firm's CEO, Chip Wilson, is an avowed Rand fan. So are the current corporate chiefs at Exxon, Sears, the BB & T Bank in North Carolina and the funky Whole Foods chain.

And of course, there's Alan Greenspan, chairman of the Federal Reserve from 1987 to 2006, who started out in the 1950s as Rand's star disciple and never in the course of his career was to abjure the special relationship.

Rand and the Mindset of the Right

Randthought, which I discuss in my book *On Nabokov, Ayn Rand and the Libertarian Mind*, serves as a major doctrinal component within the mindset of the libertarian, the latter being the most significant American ideological development of the last 35 years.

The title of a 1971 book by Jerome Tuccille (a libertarian journalist and Libertarian Party candidate for governor of New York State in 1974) says all: It Usually Begins with Ayn Rand. Rand's fan base has since grown to include Paul Ryan, the GOP's 2012 vice-presidential nominee, who in 2005 openly credited Rand with his having entered government service and who reportedly has had his staffers read the market guru's books.

Rand did not invent libertarianism. The thinking, sans the name, had been around since at least the 1920s. And her contemporaries, economists such as Milton Friedman and the so-called Austrian School, gave the set of ideas academic standing and respectability. In Rand's truculent fiction, however, an abstract theory effectively took on flesh via dashing heroes and unabashed hero worship, vivid myths and technological magic, page-turning suspense and torrid, violent scx. For every studious reader of economist Friedrich von Hayek, there are dozens, perhaps hundreds of eager devourers of Rand.

Curiously, an aging Rand loathed libertarians, attacked them as "scum," "hippies of the right" and "a monstrous, disgusting bunch of people." She hated them in great measure because, in her view, they had adopted her economic principles yet ignored her total "philosophy." (Rand also disliked any situation over which she couldn't exercise personal control.)

Her heirs and successors in the so-called Objectivist camp have since waged a kind of sectarian cold war with libertarians. One thinks of the split between Stalinists and Trotskyists or between Social Democrats and Communists.

Meanwhile the libertarians themselves have gone their merry way with their political party (the nation's third largest) and Tea Parties, and with their myriad think tanks and media organs.

The GOP's Fraught Affair with Rand

In the interim, starting with Ronald Reagan, the GOP has absorbed selected aspects of the rhetoric and larger aims of the libertarian purists (much as the New Deal did once pick and choose rhetoric and programs from the socialist left). At the same time, official party conservatism took to cultivating the evangelical Christian sectors, marshaling issues such as abortion and evolution in an aggressive bid to gain favor with fundamentalist voters.

In addition, picking up from the "Southern Strategy" of Republicans in the 1970s who wooed Southern Democrats by catering to racial tensions, candidates and publicists now play on continuing resentment over the Civil War defeat and the Civil Rights struggles. They deflect blame onto "Big Government" for any and all ills, much as libertarians and Randians are wont to do. The result is a marriage of convenience, an uneasy alliance between a pro-market, secular Right and the older, faith-based forces who make common cause against a perceived common enemy.

Rand, ironically, was an outspoken atheist, a fact that eventually led VP candidate Paul Ryan to publicly repudiate her "atheist philosophy," claiming disingenuously that his once-touted Randianism was merely an "urban legend," and that, as a Catholic, his thought came rather from St Thomas Aquinas.

Still, whatever these doctrinal differences, Rand's vision will continue to provide inspiration and intellectual ammunition for the foot soldiers of US conservatism, libertarian or otherwise.

In many respects, America is becoming—in echo of the title of a book by journalist Gary Weiss—an "Ayn Rand Nation."

American Voters Favor Democrats and Republicans, Making Third Parties Unviable

Marshall Terrill

Marshall Terrill is a media relations and strategic communications reporter for ASU Now, Arizona State University's campus news website. He is a former reporter for the East Valley Tribune *and an author of seventeen books.*

Not since the 1960s has the United States been so divided, largely split into two political camps.

But what if a third major political party emerged in the US? Would it lead to more nuanced political discourse? Is a third major party even possible, or is the two-party system "baked in" to the United States' existing election laws and legislative rules?

ASU Now spoke with Sarah Shair-Rosenfield, a professor in Arizona State University's School of Politics and Global Studies whose research focuses on the politics of electoral reform, to discuss this possibility.

Question: How likely is it for a three-or-more-party system to emerge in this country at some point?
Answer: It is difficult to predict, though the odds are not high. It's easy to assume that voter practices and norms surrounding elections—that people typically vote for either Democrats or Republicans—are the reason for this. But the actual electoral rules structuring congressional elections are one of the main sources of why the two-party system remains so strong.

We have what are called "winner take all" electoral districts for Congress: Every electoral district (House and Senate) has one seat available, and the winner is the person who gets the largest number of votes in that district, even if that number isn't a majority. This type of system nearly always produces two major parties—political scientists refer to this as "Duverger's Law." This is true even if third parties occasionally are able to break through in seat victories in a few districts, like when Green candidates do really well in elections in particular cities. This effect is compounded by the fact that there are really very few limits on campaign finance contributions and fundraising. This favors existing parties and incumbent candidates, so smaller parties may at best see only limited gains in the long run.

Q: Is our government able to deal with something akin to what we see in other countries where a third or fourth party may hold substantial numbers of seats?

A: To my knowledge, there's nothing in the Constitution or enabling legislation that prevents a coalition government from forming in the US. If a third party emerged, like a Progressive Left or a separate Tea Party, and their candidates won House or Senate seats, there isn't anything keeping them from caucusing with the Democrats or Republicans to form a majority to pass laws or joining the cabinet of a Democratic or Republican president to put those laws into practice.

But the big challenge for a multi-party US Congress is the fact that the US has what scholars of comparative politics would call relatively "undisciplined" legislative parties. In other words, while many other countries' legislatures have either formal or informal rules in place to encourage or force party members into voting on bills along party lines, the US Congress has little in comparison. That means that individual US legislators can basically vote on bills as they please from issue to issue, rather than having to vote with their co-partisans. While such individuals might be portrayed or viewed as "defectors" or "traitors" on those issues by their national party leaders, they might also come across to their constituents as "sticking to their principles." Without other penalties or incentives in place to keep them from voting against their own party, this individualistic aspect of US legislative behavior sometimes makes it difficult for even two parties to come to consensus and govern.

It isn't clear how adding a third or fourth party would really affect this, since those parties presumably wouldn't have any more "disciplined" members in Congress. I guess the point is that ungovernability in Congress doesn't necessarily stem just from having two parties who rarely see eye-to-eye on policy.

Q: Have we seen the successful rise of an outside third or fourth party anywhere in the world?

A: The most notable are in the United Kingdom and Canada, which both have similar electoral rules as the US has, including "winner take all" electoral districts for their national legislatures. Both historically have had two parties at any given time. However, both have also had successful third and fourth parties to varying degrees since the mid-20th century. In both cases those parties had to compete for decades to make big enough gains and establish themselves as viable opponents and coalition partners.

Q: In your opinion, would it be healthier for this country to have a three-party structure given how divisive we've become as a nation?

A: I think it's pretty clear from recent US elections that a lot of people are unhappy with what they see as the status quo of the Democratic and Republican party platforms and policies. I do think that if both parties faced viable challengers, it would probably force them to more seriously reevaluate their current policy preferences and strategies, though whether they would actually change what they do once in office might be more limited. (What parties do to get elected versus what they do once they are in office is rarely the same thing.) But I'm not sure that simply adding another party or two would solve a lot of the problems of political polarization we've seen in the US in recent years. I say this because a lot of other countries with rising polarization in the electorate have more than two political parties, so it's pretty clear that having more parties doesn't necessarily reduce the potential for more fixed or extreme political positions to emerge.

I think the healthiest thing would be to try to figure out ways to remind members of both parties in Congress that their jobs are to make policy and govern this country, not just serve their constituents or voting base or party elites. That doesn't really have anything to do with how many parties there are; that has to do with the kinds of individuals we elect as well as the fact that there will always be another election they are looking forward to.

Third-Party Candidates Are Often Single-Issue Campaigners, and This Does Not Benefit Democracy

Neal Lawson

Neal Lawson is the director of Compass, a British center-left advocacy group. The group aims to form political alliances that support equality, sustainability, and democracy.

Must politics disappoint? This is the public affairs question of our age. Our economy is still in crisis, those who are least to blame are paying the highest price, and our environment is heading towards disaster. How is anything ever going to change?

We already know what needs to change. The economy must be made to serve the interests of people and the planet. These always inseparable interests coalesce around polices like a real green new deal, a financial transaction tax to stop wild speculation, and the breakup of the banks to end the "too big to fail" culture. Then a living wage, ratios to control runaway executive pay and a shorter working week. A myriad of other desirable ideas could be added.

The problem is that no one knows how things might change. The political parties merge into one another. Deep in the subtext real differences exist, but they don't amount to much in practice. That's because the old parties on their own are incapable of making the transformational change that's needed.

Power and formal politics have been separated. Increasingly, power exists in two places. First, it is found at the level of global financial flows—over which national governments have little, if any, purchase. When investment decisions became the preserve of rootless private corporations, so demands for low taxes and free markets became irresistible. Control of the economy was severely reduced and democracy became the servant of capital.

"The Failure of Politics Won't Be Solved by Single-Issue Campaigners," by Neal Lawson, Guardian News & Media Limited, June 17, 2013. Reprinted by permission.

As a consequence there is a pervasive feeling that our lives are beyond our control. Decisions are made elsewhere. And nothing any national politician is saying or doing will change that. The story of the last 40 years has been a gradually diminished party political system. Because of their ebbing power no party will dominate, and coalitions will be the rule not the exception. Even if Labour were to win the next election, it's likely to be with 35% of those who vote, or 20% of the voting population. How can we create a responsible capitalism from such a narrow base?

But, in tandem, something equally important is happening. Power, as well as being globalised, is bubbling up from the self-organising grassroots. A culture of self-confidence in our views, voices and abilities is being enabled as the internet, social media and older organising techniques help people create new sources of influence.

This means the BNP was not defeated by legislation but by the Hope Not Hate campaign; the living wage is not an act of parliament but down to the organising skills of Citizens UK; tax avoidance isn't a national agenda item because of the Treasury but the actions of UK Uncut. It is the disability movement that has drawn our attention to the unfair and undignified tests disabled people now face to obtain the support they need; gay marriage is becoming a reality because gays and lesbians demanded it; and it is black youth who have highlighted the grossly disproportionate stop and search policy they frequently endure. What all these movements and campaigns have in common is that they are driven from below; often involving democratic and non-hierarchical structures. This is where their power comes from.

But these are mostly single issues, and the multiple crises we face demand joined-up answers. The political parties we can't live with, we also can't live without. The urgent task at hand is to construct a politics that not only joins the concerns of all of us who seek a much more equal, sustainable and democratic world—a good society—but which finds a way of linking formal and informal politics.

But change is complex. No single issue or party can usher in a better future alone. Formal, vertical parties are going to have to work together, and also find ways to embrace the energy and idealism of this new (and not so new), informal, bottom-up politics. So the challenge to the parties is to democratise internally and practise pluralism externally. The challenge to the movements is to shift beyond single issues and join forces to tackle the root causes of markets that are too free or too powerful, and states that are too remote or too intrusive.

The defining political trait of the future will be an "open tribalism." This recognises that people start from a party or a single-issue bias but that to succeed they are going to have to be pluralistic and respectful of others. Change will come from consensus, not control.

If we are to flourish as fully rounded human beings then the dividing lines are clear. They are between those who want to protect their privilege and the rest of us who want no more than decency, respect and some semblance of economic and environmental balance, but also between the old, closed tribes of heavy-handed politics and the new, open movements for change. The ideas, policies and structures to build a good society lie all around us. It is in our gift to construct them in a way that, in the words of the academic and writer Raymond Williams, "makes hope possible, rather than despair convincing."

Because Socialism Is Considered Un-American, It Is Unlikely a Democratic Socialist Would Be Elected President

Oana Godeanu-Kenworthy

Oana Godeanu-Kenworthy is an associate teaching professor of American studies at Miami University in Ohio, where she is also an affiliate of the Havighurst Center for Russian and Post-Soviet Studies.

Bernie Sanders has emerged as the Democratic front-runner in the race for the presidential nomination.

Yet even some left-leaning pundits and publications are concerned about what they see as Sanders' potential lack of electability.

Sanders is a Democratic Socialist. And the label "socialist" is a political liability in American culture. According to a Gallup poll released on Feb. 11, 2020, only 45% of Americans would vote for a socialist.

I am a scholar of American culture with an interest in the relationship between political ideologies and popular culture. In my research, I have found that this antipathy toward socialism may not be an accident: American identity today is strongly tied to an image of capitalism crafted and advertised by the Ad Council and American corporate interests over decades, often with the support of the US government.

Business and Government Solidarity

In 1942, a group of advertising and industry executives created the War Advertising Council, to promote the war effort. The government compensated the companies that created or donated

"How Socialism Became Un-American Through the Ad Council's Propaganda Campaigns," by Oana Godeanu-Kenworthy, The Conversation Media Group Ltd., February 27, 2020. http://theconversation.com/how-socialism-became-un-american -through-the-ad-councils-propaganda-campaigns-132335. Licensed under CC BY-ND 4.0.

ads by allowing them to deduct some of their costs from their taxable incomes.

Renamed the Ad Council in 1943, the organization applied the same wartime persuasive techniques of advertising and psychological manipulation during the Cold War years, the post-war period when the geopolitical rivalry between the US, the USSR and their respective allies raged. One of their goals: promoting the virtues of capitalism and free enterprise in America while simultaneously demonizing the alternative—socialism—which was often conflated with communism.

Government propaganda at home portrayed the communist USSR as godless, tyrannical and antithetical to individual freedoms. As a counterpoint, America became everything the Soviet Union was not.

This link between capitalism and American national identity was advertised through a sophisticated, corporate effort as efficient and ubiquitous as state-driven propaganda behind the Iron Curtain.

The campaigns used the ideological divisions of the Cold War to emphasize the relevance of their message. In a 1948 report, the Ad Council explained its goal to the public: "The world today is engaged in a colossal struggle to determine whether freedom or statism will dominate."

Extolling Capitalism's Virtues

The campaigns started as a public-private partnership. At the end of World War II, the government worried about the spread of communism at home. Business interests worried about government regulations and about the rising popularity of unions. The Cold War provided both parties with a shared enemy.

In 1947, President Truman asked the Ad Council to organize the Freedom Train Campaign, focusing on the history of America's political freedoms. Paramount Pictures, US Steel, DuPont, General Electric and Standard Oil provided financial support. For two years the train crisscrossed the nation, carrying original documents that included the Bill of Rights and the Constitution.

The media industry donated $40 million in free space and air time in the first year of the campaign. The Department of Commerce and the Department of Labor contributed about half a million dollars toward the production costs for a 20-page booklet.

That booklet used data provided by the departments of Commerce and Labor and Charles Schulz's "Peanuts" comic strips to explain the benefits of America's economic system. The system was again presented as a foundational freedom protected by a Constitution whose goal was to "maintain a climate in which people could work, invest, and prosper."

By 1979, 13 million copies had been distributed to schools, universities, libraries, civic organizations and workplaces.

Echoes Now?

For four decades, the Cold War provided a simple good-vs.-evil axis that consolidated the association between freedom, American-ness and free-enterprise capitalism.

The business community, independently and through the Ad Council, funded massive top-down economic education programs that shaped American perceptions of business and government and of capitalism and socialism.

The Cold War ended 30 years ago, but its cultural structures and divisions endure—perhaps, even, in the responses of some Americans to Bernie Sanders' socialism.

CHAPTER 4

Do Third Parties Have a Future in the United States?

Overview: History Shows That Third Parties Can Impact Politics in the US

Julia Foodman

Julia Foodman is a former communications intern for FairVote. She has also served as a legislative campaigns intern for the Montana Democratic Party and a communications and field officer for a congressional campaign in California.

W hile third party presidential candidates typically only win small portions of the overall vote, they are often blamed for altering the outcome of elections. This perception could be solved very easily with ranked choice voting (RCV), either in states today by statute or for the national popular vote through national action.

Even before the defined establishment of the modern Democratic and Republican parties, there have been many third party candidates who have run outside of the typical party structure. These third party candidates typically receive a small portion of the popular vote and no votes from the Electoral College, though there are numerous exceptions.

In July of presidential election years, the Democratic National Convention and the Republican National Convention convene to select their nominees. However, many lesser-known parties also meet and nominate a candidate. Today, the Libertarian and Green parties are the most notable to do so, but, historically, a handful of other parties including the Constitution, Prohibition, States Rights, Populist, and Socialist parties have held conventions to send a presidential and vice-presidential nominee to the ballot.

Since the dominant two-party system has solidified, no third party candidates has won a presidential election. Nonetheless, historically they have played a critical role in forcing major parties to cater to the issues that people care about the most. Had ranked

"A History of Third Party and Independent Presidential Candidates," by Julia Foodman, FairVote, July 16, 2019. Reprinted by permission.

choice voting been implemented during our previous 58 American presidential elections, our history of presidents would likely look different. We will examine our diverse history of third party candidates who, while not winning the presidency themselves, often affected the outcome.

2016

In the last presidential election, a whopping 32 candidates vied for the presidency, with the least competitive of them receiving just 332 votes nationwide.

Libertarian Gary Johnson, former Governor of New Mexico, garnered 3.3 percent of the vote. While that may not seem significant, he did accrue nearly 4.4 million votes, more than a million more than the total by which Hillary Clinton won the popular vote. Likewise, Jill Stein of the Green Party got 1.1 percent of the vote, making her the first fourth-place finisher to breach the one-million-vote mark since 1948.

14 states were won with less than half the votes, with half of those states won by Clinton and half by Trump—including such battlegrounds as Arizona, Florida, Michigan, Pennsylvnia and Wisconsin. While, at first glance, it might appear that, if Johnson and Stein votes had gone to Clinton, she would be president, we must remember that not all such voters would have all voted for Clinton. Many Johnson voters may have voted for Donald Trump instead given the ideological closeness of libertarianism and conservative economic stances and Johnson's two terms as a Republican governor of New Mexico.

A more likely scenario would have been some combination of Stein's and Johnson's voters voting for Clinton, though we will never be able to draw a definite conclusion of that potential outcome because RCV was not in place. What we can say is that the election results could potentially have been different, as neither candidate reached 50 percent of the vote.

2000

Similar to the 2016 election, the candidate who won the popular vote did not win the election. Because Republican George W. Bush won in the Electoral College by only four votes and won the key battleground of Florida by only 537 votes, third parties did play a role in the outcome. In total, third party candidates garnered 138,063 votes in Florida, with the Green Party's Ralph Nader accruing over 97,488 of those votes. Had Florida voters had the opportunity to rank their vote, the final results in the state may have looked quite different.

1996, 1992

Bill Clinton won the 1996 and 1992 elections with less than fifty percent of the vote, which RCV is designed to prevent. In these election years, the Reform Party's Ross Perot ran successful campaigns, garnering 18.7 percent and 9.2 percent, respectively. Though Reform Party ideals align more closely with the Republican platform, independent analyses indicate that Perot drew equally from Republicans and Democrats. Therefore, we cannot say definitely that the election results would have been different had RCV been implemented—but we can say that in 1992, only a single state (Clinton's home state of Arkansas) was won with more than half the votes.

Perot passed away on Tuesday, July 9, and is the most successful third party candidate in modern American history.

1980

FairVote's co-founder John B. Anderson started the year as a Republican candidate who had served in Congress for 20 years. After Ronald Reagan gained the upper hand in the nomination, Anderson left the party to run as an independent to uphold his tradition as a "Rockefeller Republican." Early on he polled over 20 percent and secured a role in one debate, but ultimately won 6.6 percent—more than six times the total for the Libertarian Party ticket that included David Koch, one of the two Koch brothers who have played a major role in Republican politics in recent years. Reagan won more than 50 percent nationally, but only 26 states were won with more than half the votes.

1968

This election was unlike any previously seen in the country. George Wallace, widely known for his quote, "Segregation now, segregation tomorrow, segregation forever," ran with the American Independent Party because his pro-segregation policies had been rejected by the mainstream of the Democratic Party.

Wallace, with 12.9 percent of the popular vote, ended up winning five southern states, accruing 46 electoral college votes. Republican Richard Nixon won 43.2 percent of the popular vote but 56.1 percent of the electoral college; Democrat Hubert Humphrey won 42.6 percent of the popular vote but only 35.5 percent of the electoral college.

It should be noted that Wallace did not expect to win the election; his strategy was to prevent either major party candidate from winning a preliminary majority in the Electoral College. He had his electors pledge to vote not necessarily for him but for whomever he directed them to support. His objective was not to move the election into the US House of Representatives, but rather to give himself the bargaining power to determine the winner. Though he was ultimately unsuccessful, he managed to prevent either party from winning a popular vote majority. A shift of just 1.55 percent in California would have given Wallace the swing power in the Electoral College he sought.

After the election, Republican President Richard Nixon pushed Congress to abolish the Electoral College—with Hubert Humphrey's support—because Wallace had attempted to do something the founding fathers would not have anticipated.

1912

Republican Theodore Roosevelt had served as president from 1901 to 1909, and William Howard Taft had won the 1908 Republican presidential nomination with Roosevelt's support. Displeased with Taft's actions as president, Roosevelt challenged Taft in 1912.

After being denied the Republican nomination in an era before presidential primaries, Roosevelt rallied his progressive supporters and launched a third party bid. Roosevelt's Progressive Party, nicknamed the "Bull Moose Party," lost the election but marked the most successful third party bid in history, winning 27.4 percent of the vote. Taft, the incumbent president, did not perform as well, winning 23.7 percent. The Socialist Party also had a successful race this year, as Socialist nominee Eugene V. Debs secured 6 percent.

Four candidates made significant waves this election. In one potential scenario with RCV, Debs would have been eliminated and his second choice votes would have gone to Roosevelt or Wilson. Then Taft would've been eliminated, and his second choice votes probably would not have gone to Woodrow Wilson (who ultimately won), but to Roosevelt instead. Evidently, the results could have been drastically different.

Notably, talk of second choice voting grew markedly after this election, with the Nebraska Bull Moose Party actually endorsing it in its official platform.

1892

In 1891, the American Farmers' Alliances met with delegates from labor and reform groups in Cincinnati, Ohio, to discuss the formation of a new political party. They formed the People's Party, commonly known as the Populists. James B. Weaver of the Populist Party carried five states, accruing 8.5 percent of the popular vote, while winner Grover Cleveland earned 46 percent. If RCV had been implemented, this election would have had a winner with majority support.

1860

In the 1860 election, no candidate reached 40 percent of the vote. At a time when the nation was so divided, the vote matched the political climate. Republican Abraham Lincoln won the election; however, Democratic voters were divided between Northern Democrat Stephen A. Douglas and Southern Democrat John C. Breckinridge. Together they accrued 47.6 percent of the vote, significantly more than Lincoln. John Bell of Constitution Union got 12.6 percent. While Lincoln won only 39.7 percent of the national popular vote, he did win more than half the votes in northern states that together had more than half of the Electoral College.

While ranked choice voting within the Electoral College system would not have prevented Lincoln's victory and the resulting civil war, it could have provided a clearer picture of the fault lines dividing the country.

1856

Former Whig President Millard Fillmore, running on the American Party platform, won 21.5 percent of the vote in this election, winning only Maryland. Second choice votes could have either pushed the winner, James Buchanan, who earned 45.3 percent, or runner-up John Fremont, who won 33.11 percent, over the 50 percent majority margin.

1848

Democrat Martin Van Buren was president from 1837–1841. After getting booted out of office, he ran a failed campaign in 1848 as a candidate for the anti-slavery Free Soil Party. Van Buren won over ten percent of the vote, preventing the Whig candidate (eventual winner Zachary Taylor) or Democratic candidate Lewis Cass from earning support from half the country's electorate.

1844

In 1844, pro-slavery candidate James K. Polk ran against soft abolitionist Henry Clay and hard-line abolitionist James Birney. While Polk ended up winning the election, Clay and Birney did split votes. Most notably, this occurred in New York, where Birney received 15,812 votes but Polk beat Clay by only 5,106 votes. If ranked choice voting had been implemented in this election, it is quite possible the country would have elected a different president and, most importantly, taken a different tack in regards to slavery. Polk beat Clay in New York by 5,106 votes, yet Birney received 15,812 votes.

1788–1844

Sixty-nine Electoral College votes unanimously elected George Washington as president of the United States in 1788. Since then, candidates, political parties, electors, and the very fabric of our country have evolved significantly. As early as 1824, John Quincy Adams was chosen by the House of Representatives as president after earning only 31 percent of popular votes compared to Andrew Jackson's 41 percent.

Recent Electoral Trends Suggest Voters Are Willing to Look Beyond Traditional Democratic and Republican Candidates

Peggy Nash

Peggy Nash is a senior adviser to the Ryerson University Dean of Arts and co-founder of the Ryerson University Women in the House program. She is also a former member of the Canadian Parliament.

The youngest woman ever elected to the United States Congress, Democrat Alexandria Ocasio-Cortez, is a force to contend with. With clear and forthright language, she speaks the truth of people's reality—and one that is rooted in her own lived experience.

With a megawatt smile and a wink to her demographic, she also has verve and style. Two days after she debated 10-term incumbent congressman Joe Crowley last June during the primaries, she tweeted her lipstick shade, which promptly sold out on the Stila and Sephora web sites.

Social Media Powerhouse

AOC, as she is popularly known, has more than three million followers on her Instagram account and four million follow her @AOC Twitter account, a 600 per cent increase from last June and more than 2.6 million gained in the past eight months. How does she do it?

Unlike other politicians, she speaks the language of now, especially to her generation. She is down-to-earth and personable. In some of her video postings, she shares her life both in Congress and at home, as if you are getting caught up with a friend.

"Alexandria Ocasio-Cortez Is Shaking Up Old Politics with Her New Style," by Peggy Nash, The Conversation Media Group Ltd., May 22, 2019. https://theconversation.com /alexandria-ocasio-cortez-is-shaking-up-old-politics-with-her-new-style-116948. Licensed under CC BY ND 4.0.

As a former member of Parliament in Canada, I can tell you, it would be a mistake to brush AOC off as just the flavour of the month. She is no lightweight. AOC's social media presence is based on trust and authenticity. Her messages are about taking action. And they are a perfect foil to what US President Donald Trump represents.

The Fury of the US Public

On Nov. 8, 2016, the US elected a president who bragged about sexual assault and racism. In addition, right-wing parties were on the rise in Europe and inequality in the US had intensified. People were angry.

The Women's March on Washington the day after Trump's inauguration has been called the largest one-day demonstration in US history. There followed Trump's attacks on immigrants and refugees and the spectacle of the Brett Kavanaugh hearings and the testimony of Christine Blasey Ford. The proceedings echoed the Clarence Thomas hearings, which discounted the testimony and courage of law professor Anita Hill. The committee even had some of the same members as a generation earlier.

The fury of the American public led to the greatest number of diverse candidates to ever run in the US midterm elections last fall. Many of those candidates lost. But several of them won.

Indigenous, queer, Muslim, Black and women candidates are now represented in greater numbers than ever before. And many of those who lost had a strong showing. This means they have teams in place, voters identified, name recognition and often money in the bank. They just have not won yet.

AOC's Appeal Drives Republicans Crazy

Enter Alexandria Ocasio-Cortez. She campaigned in a safe Democrat seat but argued that milquetoast Democrats were enabling the growing divide between the one per cent and the 99 per cent. Her campaign video blew up the internet and thrust her into the lives of New Yorkers like a force of nature. That she could beat a congressman as powerful as Crowley shows that she tapped into the reality of her fellow New Yorkers.

Most importantly, Ocasio-Cortez began shaking up the Washington establishment with her bold proposal to reshape America with her Green New Deal, in the spirit of President Roosevelt's New Deal to get the US out of the Great Depression. Her stimulus plan aims to phase in renewable energy sources and rebalance the social and economic pie in the United States with a proposed tax hike on the richest Americans.

She is also advocating for free tuition, universal single-payer health care, a job guarantee with decent wages and benefits and transitioning the US economy to 100 per cent renewable energy sources. Her vision is far to the left of the cautious and ultimately uninspiring Hillary Clinton, but current Democratic presidential hopefuls are falling over themselves to endorse her plan.

Both her audacious goals and her bold style drive her Republican opponents crazy. They believe that her socialist politics will lose the Democrats the votes of more moderate Americans so they have fixed a negative spotlight on her.

Alternatively, AOC might just be tapping into the anxiety of Americans across party lines as they struggle to make ends meet while harbouring anxieties about climate change.

Women's Rising Power in Politics

One thing is clear, Ocasio-Cortez is making an imprint on a generation of Americans, especially young women, with a message to get informed, get organized and get involved. Young women in the US are becoming more politically engaged, from the Parkland students to the #MeToo movement.

Here in Canada, we can see a similar pattern in the number and diversity of candidates running for election and applying to programs like Women in House, Daughters of the Vote and the Institute for Future Legislators at Ryerson University and UBC.

To old-style politicians, AOC supporters say "step up or step aside." She may not be a vampire slayer or have an army or a quiver of arrows. Nevertheless, she's as fierce a fighter inspiring young Americans to seek change as any cultural superhero, a combination of Buffy, Okoye and Katniss.

In addition to her bold platform, her real superpower seems to be her fearless confrontation, her spirited style and her ability to inspire others to action.

The test will be if it continues to spread beyond the Bronx.

Allowing Third-Party Candidates to Participate in Presidential Debates Would Give Them a Fair Chance

Ann Ravel

Ann Ravel is former chair of the Federal Election Commission. She is also an attorney and a 2020 Democratic candidate for the California State Senate.

This year marks the 60th anniversary of the first televised presidential debate. Like the contest between John F. Kennedy and Richard M. Nixon, debates today play a critical role in determining who will occupy the White House. They inform Americans of the positions, values and ideas of the candidates—and simply let us see how they perform under pressure.

No one has a chance of becoming president without participating in the fall debates. So ensuring a fair method of determining who can be on the stage is crucial to the integrity of our elections. A subject of controversy for years has been the systematic exclusion of third-party and independent candidates. Their absence regularly—and unfairly—tips the scales in favor of certain candidates over others.

Next week, the Court of Appeals for the District of Columbia will hear a lawsuit against the Federal Election Commission (FEC), which I used to chair. The suit, filed by the non-profit group Level the Playing Field, argues that debate access rules set by the Commission on Presidential Debates (CPD) favor Democratic and Republican nominees and systematically exclude independents and third-party candidates. The law requires that the CPD use non-partisan, objective criteria.

The suit, which I support, will determine if any qualified American can ever successfully run for president outside the two-party nominating system. It will be heard by a three-judge

"Third Parties Deserve Shot at Debate Stage," by Ann Ravel, RealClearHoldings,LLC, February 21, 2020. Reprinted by permission.

panel consisting of Judges Gregory Katsas, Cornelia Pillard, and A. Raymond Randolph.

In 1987, after the withdrawal of the League of Women Voters, control of the debates was assumed by the two major political parties, which jointly formed the CPD. That organization requires participants to receive at least 15% support in a series of opinion polls shortly before the debates—a rule long subject to criticism.

As the chair of the FEC, which has oversight over some aspects of the debates, I called for a review of the debate-access rules. Why? Because since the rules' adoption in 2000, no candidate unaffiliated with either the Democrat or Republican parties has ever surmounted the 15% hurdle.

Serious presidential candidates need to begin their campaigns at least 18 months before Election Day. How then can an independent gain early backing without some credible path into the final fall debates? Unfortunately, my colleagues disagreed. They refused even to hold a review, and the FEC continues to this day to ignore the consequences of maintaining the status quo.

Voters consistently say they prefer a more inclusive debate. The two major parties disagree. They argue that because alternative candidates are unlikely to win, they do not belong on the debate stage. But I am convinced that the absence of just such candidates harms America's development as a nation.

As legal scholar Keith Darren Eisner argues, this narrow conception of "who belongs" misses the ways in which "third-party and independent candidates play a vital role in the American political process, a role independent of electoral success." Without alternative candidates, compelling ideas may be lost to the American people.

Simple rule changes are easily available. For example, Mitch Daniels, president of Purdue University and a former member of the CPD, advocated dropping the arbitrary 15% hurdle. One option would be to include the top three polling candidates as debate participants. This seems reasonable and fair, given that a monthly Gallup survey shows consistently that independents far outnumber either Democrats or Republicans.

Americans want to see other candidates on the debate stage even if those candidates have little chance to win. In 1980, when the League of Women Voters asked likely voters whether they thought John Anderson, an independent who was running against Ronald Reagan and then-President Jimmy Carter, should be included in the first presidential debate, 63% said yes—even though fewer than 15% said they would vote for Anderson on Election Day.

In 2000, more than half of American adults told pollsters that they wished Ralph Nader had been invited to participate in the first debate. In the 2016 election, nearly half of voters supported including Green Party nominee Jill Stein and Libertarian Gary Johnson in the first debate; only 39% wanted the debate restricted to the two major-party candidates. Another 2016 poll found that nine in 10 people would be just as likely or more likely to watch a debate that was "more inclusive of independent or third-party candidates."

When alternative candidates are denied the opportunity to promote forward-thinking policies at the most widely viewed political event of election season, the entire country suffers.

When the major candidates debate only each another, rather than also having to respond to the ideas of other contenders, they can ignore any issues on which they already agree. The result is that voters are hindered from learning where the candidates stand on the full range of issues and, more generally, from encountering innovative policy ideas they may not have considered before.

By contrast, in 1992, the last time an independent candidate participated in the presidential debates, Ross Perot raised balancing the federal budget as a top issue. Although Perot failed to carry a single state, voters responded favorably to the idea, and under the winner, Bill Clinton, the budget was balanced in 1998 for the first time in 29 years.

The success of the Level the Playing Field litigation is important to maintaining a robust political process. Unless the Commission on Presidential Debates changes its access rules, Americans won't have the real choice they deserve.

A Multiparty System Would Strengthen American Democracy

George Cheung

George Cheung is a program director for the Joyce Foundation's Democracy Program. He previously directed two nonprofit advocacy organizations and worked in civil rights law enforcement, focusing on fair housing compliance for state agencies in Rhode Island, Massachusetts, and Washington.

P ro-democracy reformers, activists, and funders in the United States tend to focus on increasing voter turnout by decreasing the barriers to voter registration and casting a ballot. But in doing so, they're missing something important: the broken two-party system. In the market economy consumers have a plethora of choices for virtually every good and service. How, then, when it comes to US general elections, can one expect the American voter to be excited with two choices at best—or, as in most Congressional and many state legislative races, no meaningful choice at all?

Reducing barriers to voting is a good idea, but what's really needed is a shift to a multi-party system through proportional representation; many comparative studies suggest that such a shift would lead to an increase in voter turnout of between 9 and 12 percent.

Young People Want More Choices

As a generation, Millennials are more ethnically diverse, hold more progressive views on social issues, and are more likely to favor a strong role for government than previous cohorts. How does this translate into affiliating with political parties? A poll conducted by the Pew Research Center in early 2014, found that about half of Millennials did not identify with either the Democratic or

"Strengthening Democracy by Embracing a Multi-Party System," by George Cheung, Stanford University, February 4, 2016. Reprinted by permission.

Republican political party, an increase from 38 percent in 2004. Further, only 31 percent of Millennials saw big differences between the two parties, compared to 43 percent of all respondents in the same survey.

These data suggest a desire for alternative choices. In a NBC News/Survey Monkey poll of Democratic voters released in mid-October, 2015, 54 percent of young people backed socialist Bernie Sanders compared to just 26 percent for Hillary Clinton. Under a proportional representation system, many of these young people might gravitate towards a Social Democratic, Green, or Working Families Party. Without any significant change to the US electoral system, we should expect continued political disaffection by young people, barring the exceptional presidential candidate who is able to inspire and mobilize.

Strategic Voting, the Spoiler Effect, and the GOP Civil War

"But we have lots of political parties." That's what one Democratic Party activist told me in a recent conversation about the merits of a multi-party system. He was technically correct; however, the US electoral system, often called "first past the post" or "winner-take-all" system, inherited from British colonialism, is set up to give just two parties any meaningful chance to win elections and govern. In the United States, voters who favor a non-major party candidate must decide between casting a strategic vote for the "lesser of two evils" or casting a vote for their first choice, which could perversely help their least favored candidate to win. (Meanwhile, the vast majority of democracies in other countries have adopted true multi-party systems, mostly as a way for elections to truly reflect the views of voters.)

Consider how current non-major parties have fared in recent US elections. On the left, the Working Families Party arguably has the most momentum. Launched in 1998 by a coalition of labor unions, community-based organizations, and remnants of the New Party, the Working Families Party is electorally active in a handful of states. In New York, where fusion voting allows two or more political parties on a ballot to list the same candidate, the party has been able to claim victories of endorsed candidates including Governor Andrew Cuomo and New York City Mayor Bill de Blasio. However, only one candidate, Edwin Gomes, has ever been able to win election solely as the nominee of the Working Families Party; the race was for State Senate in Connecticut, and Gomes had formerly represented the same district as a Democrat.

Without a change to the electoral system, the Working Families Party will struggle to win a single seat in any legislative chamber—that's a far cry from being able to channel energy from protest movements such as Occupy Wall Street into electoral power.

On the right, there's the very different dynamic of the Tea Party. Since the 2008 elections, Tea Party candidates do not run under the party label. Instead, they typically challenge establishment Republicans by offering what they tout as a more ideologically pure alternative. Successful Tea Party house candidates have formed the Freedom Caucus, which generally blocks the Republican Caucus from compromising with Democrats. Under a multi-party system, the Tea Party could function as a separate party, distinct from the pro-business, pro-immigration Republican Party of previous generations. That structure would not necessarily increase voter turnout among conservatives, but it could very well result in a more functional Congress where compromise is not taboo.

Increasing Competition and Enhancing Voting Rights

The lack of competitive races is a sad hallmark of the US electoral system. In most states, the decennial process of redistricting results is effectively an incumbency protection plan. Races, at least in the general election, are largely pro forma. I've voted in four states since first registering in 1991. I can recall voting in only one Congressional election where the incumbent didn't win in a landslide.

Elections in a multi-party system are structurally more competitive. With single member districts in a two-party race (districts that elect one representative to office), a candidate needs 50 percent plus one vote to win a seat. In three-member districts (which were used to elect the Illinois State Assembly for more than 100 years, until 1980), the threshold for winning one of three seats can be 30 percent or even less. A shift to multi-member districts (where more than one person is elected to office) could make virtually every district competitive, forcing all candidates to campaign aggressively and encourage voters to participate.

What's more, the increase in competitiveness would not come at the expense of voting rights. Since voters who support Democratic congressional and state legislative candidates are more concentrated in urban areas, more competitive races would mean splitting up these communities and combining them with predominantly Republican suburbs. Given that these urban communities are disproportionately composed of people of color, such a change could have a detrimental impact on minority voting rights—a difficult tradeoff. A multi-member district system could resolve the tension by offering meaningful competition but also providing a method for communities of color to elect someone of their choice. In fact, for Asian Americans, who do not have the same history of racial segregation as African Americans, a multi-member district system offers an opportunity to more easily elect their preferred candidate.

Modernizing our system of election administration is critical to removing barriers to participation and instilling confidence that each vote will be counted. But if voters do not have meaningful choices at the ballot box, why should they bother to show up?

Two-Party Politics Increases Civic Engagement and Makes a More Cohesive and Vibrant Democracy

Pietro S. Nivola

Pietro S. Nivola was a senior fellow emeritus at the Brookings Institution, an American research group. He was also an associate professor of political science at the University of Vermont and a lecturer in the government department at Harvard University.

From the steps of the Capitol on January 20th, President Barack Obama appealed for an end to the politics of "petty grievances" and "worn-out dogmas." The year 2009 was supposed to mark the dawn of a post-partisan era. With any luck, Democrats and Republicans would stop quarreling, and would finally get down to work together. The time had come, exhorted the new president drawing from Scripture, to lay "childish" polemics aside.

But childish or not, America's partisan politics have remained as stubbornly intense and polarized as ever. To paraphrase more Scripture, the lambs remain unwilling to lie down with the lions. And there are few signs of partisan swords being turned into plowshares. Far from opening a new age of bipartisan comity in the House of Representatives, the president and the Democratic majority received not a single Republican vote in their first big legislative test, the roll call on the so-called American Recovery and Reinvestment Act (the "stimulus"). More recently, not one Republican in the Senate or the House voted for the concurrent resolution on the president's budget. More, not less, of such party-line voting probably lies ahead.

So here's a heretical thought: Maybe, among the many inflated expectations that we attach to the Obama presidency and should temper, those about the advent of "post-partisanship" ought to be

"In Defense of Partisan Politics," by Pietro S. Nivola, The Brookings Institution, April 8, 2009. Reprinted by permission.

lowered, drastically. In other words, get over it. The rough-and-tumble of our party politics is here to stay. What's more—and this is even greater heresy—not everything about that fact of political life is horrible.

Majoritarianism

The Democratic and Republican parties today are each more cemented in their ideologies and more distinct than they were a generation ago. In Congress, party lines used to be blurred by the existence of so-called liberal Republicans and truly conservative Democrats. Now those factions are dwindling species. Why they are dying out is a long story that has been the object of an extensive study titled *Red and Blue Nation?* cosponsored by Brookings and the Hoover Institution at Stanford University. For present purposes, suffice it to recognize that the disputes between Republicans and Democrats are about more than "petty grievances" (though there are plenty of them, too); the party differences run deep and fundamentally reflect differing convictions held by large blocs of voters, not just their elected representatives. An example: Whereas a staggering 84 percent of Democrats seem to believe "it's the government's responsibility to make sure that everyone in the United States has adequate health care," only 34 percent of Republicans evidently concur, according to a reputable national poll taken last November.

Because both parties are more cohesive, they are also more disciplined. If you are a member of Congress and you basically agree with your party's position on most salient issues, why defect to the other side on key votes? Americans of the baby-boom generation are not accustomed to seeing this high degree of party unity. They remember the old days when the main way to do business on Capitol Hill was to cobble together ad-hoc coalitions. Want a civil rights bill? Get northern Democrats and Republican moderates on your side, and hope that you have enough votes to overpower the conservative phalanx of southern Democrats and states'-rights Republicans. Want more money for the Vietnam

War in the 1960s? Combine solid support from that bipartisan conservative bloc with plenty of other hawkish stalwarts in both parties (think reliable GOP loyalists like Everett Dirksen but also Scoop Jackson Democrats), and you'd get the funds.

Increasingly, the contemporary party system bears scant resemblance to the one that prevailed a half-century ago. What it resembles instead is politics in most other periods of American history, for example the late nineteenth century when the two parties were also internally coherent and keenly at odds. During such periods, the American parties have behaved more like political parties in parliamentary regimes—where the in-party (the governing majority) rules, and the out-party (the minority) consistently forms a loyal opposition.

Notice this distinctive feature of the parliamentary model: Not only can the majority, voting in lockstep, prevail with no help from opposition members; all it needs on board in order to legislate is a simple majority of the legislators. Supermajorities—the requirement in the US Senate to override a filibuster—are never the norm. A parliamentary system, in other words, operates much like our congressional budget reconciliation process where as little as a one-vote margin in the House and as little as 51 votes in the Senate suffice to adopt a bill.

There is much handwringing about the trend toward majoritarian—that is, parliamentary-style—politics in the United States. Democrats moaned when the GOP, led by George W. Bush, drove tax cuts through Congress on nearly a party-line vote with Vice President Cheney casting the tie-breaker. Now, Republicans will groan if the Obama administration and the Democratic congressional leadership opt to use the reconciliation procedure to ram health-care reform into law.

But is all the lamentation justified?

Accountability

One of the advantages of parliamentary democracy is that the electorate knows what to expect. What you see (or vote for) is what you get. As America becomes parliamentary, if voters elect a Republican president and congressional majority, here's a good bet: Tax cuts will be on the way. If voters elect a Democratic president and congressional majority—running on a party platform that declares universal health care to be a "moral imperative"—guess what? Health-care legislation to extend coverage will happen. Now, granted one can debate the policy merits of either party's priorities. Robotic tax-cutting runs up deficits—and so almost certainly will health care that covers everybody. But if the voters have explicitly empowered their elected officials to do either of these things, who are "we" to stand in the way?

Further, the voters have plenty of opportunity to change their minds. If they decide that mistakes are being made—or that they prefer an alternative agenda to the one being proffered by the party in power—they can throw the rascals out. Indeed, in this country, unlike practically every other democracy, the public gets a chance to entertain that option with extraordinary frequency: every two years.

Nor, from the standpoint of democratic theory, is it easy to make an airtight case for why Congress and the president should be forced to muster supermajorities to enact their most important priorities. Ours, like any sound democracy, has to balance principles of majority rule with minority rights. But a political order in which technically just over 7 percent of a legislature—that is, a sub-group that possibly represents as little as 10 percent of the population—can have the last word, as our Senate arithmetic can imply, raises serious questions of democratic accountability and even legitimacy. Let's face it; making a regular practice of putting, in effect, veto-power in the hands of a minority is hard to square with a government of the people, by the people, for the people.

The Virtues of a Choice, Not an Echo

There is one other thing to say in defense of heightened partisanship: It has succeeded in making elections more interesting.

Voters have a tendency to become indifferent and apathetic when asked to choose between alternatives that display not "a dime's worth of difference," as the old saying went about our two-party system during the heyday of bipartisan comingling.

By contrast, as Marc J. Hetherington of Vanderbilt University demonstrates in a key chapter of *Red and Blue Nation?*, voter participation has surged as the partisan divide has grown sharper.

The electorate is not turned off by the chasm, and contestation, between the parties. On the contrary, Hetherington finds, the polarized political parties have animated voters of all stripes—liberals, conservatives, and moderates. Growing civic engagement and voter turnouts are hallmarks of a vibrant democracy, not of a "broken" one.

The Two-Party System Is Durable, Rigid, and Here to Stay

Eric Black

Eric Black is a journalist who writes the "Eric Black Ink" column for MinnPost. In 2017, he won the national Sigma Delta Chi Award for online column writing from the Society of Professional Journalists.

I've cited it a few times before, but I still get a smile out of what Minnesota political analyst Wy Spano once told me was his favorite cartoon. It shows two voters, meeting on their way out of the polling place, and one says to the other: "Which one did you vote against?"

Having to vote for the lesser of two evils is an old complaint in US elections. This year it may have special resonance for Americans who find themselves with two major party nominees who spent most of this year with favorability ratings that are "under water," meaning more disapprovers than approvers. (President Obama's approval rating recently surged to just-barely-above-water status.)

Perhaps this reflects the grumpy mood of the public more than the inadequacy of the candidates. I don't mean to back-handedly endorse the idea that neither of the nominees would be a good president. But those poll ratings remind us that our American party system provides us with only two meaningful choices in most general elections.

Today, let's think outside the box for a moment and contemplate the durable rigidity and the quasi-constitutional roots of the US two-party system.

By rigid, I mean that a voter who isn't excited about either the Democrat or the Republican nominee has little choice other than giving his vote to the lesser evil, or voting for a minor party candidate who has no chance of winning—which in our system is

"Why the Same Two Parties Dominate Our Two-Party System," by Eric Black, *MinnPost*, October 8, 2012. Reprinted by permission.

sometimes called the wasted-vote syndrome—or dropping out of the electorate (as an embarrassingly large portion of our potential electorate does every cycle). I don't mean to provide non-voters with a high-minded excuse for their apathy. And, of course, a citizen can get involved with the party they prefer and try to help nominate candidates about whom they could get excited.

Most Have More Parties

But it's just a fact that most of the democracies in the world have more than two parties that play a more politically meaningful role than any third parties do in the United States (or have for more than a century). That's what I mean by durable.

The Democratic Party formed essentially out of the (Andrew) Jacksonians in the 1820s. In some tellings, the Democrats prefer to trace their roots back a little further to the party of Thomas Jefferson, which called itself the Democratic Republican Party. Fun fact (if you're as hard-up for fun as I am): In most states, the annual banquet/fundraiser for the Democratic Party is called the Jefferson-Jackson dinner. But in Minnesota, where the Democratic Party is the DFL Party, the dinner has been known for years at the Humphrey Day Dinner and has now been rechristened the Humphrey-Mondale Dinner. End of fun until further notice.

But the original historical/analytical point about durability is this (and there is nothing else like it in the world): Since the Republican Party formed in the 1850s and replaced the Whig Party as the second of the two major parties, the two-party lineup has consisted of the same two parties, Democrats and Republicans. Even in those democracies that have a two-party system, the identity of the parties changes more frequently than that.

The Republicrat duopoly is not total, but almost. At the state level, third parties have been relevant. (One of the biggest cases is the leftist Farmer-Labor Party, a Minnesota-only institution that dominated Minnesota politics for a while in 1930s, before disappearing in the '40s into a merger with the Democrats.) And the centrist Independence Party of Minnesota is probably the strongest state-based third party in the country over recent years, spinning off from the Perot movement of the 1990s and even winning one statewide race (the 1998 election of that great statesman Gov. Jesse Ventura). But the centrist party now seems to be struggling for survival, or perhaps seeking a new way back to relevance.

No one other than a Democrat or a Republican has been elected president since Whig nominee Zachary Taylor in 1848. No party other than the Democrats or the Republicans has held a majority (or anything near a majority or even a numerically significant minority) in either house of Congress since the Republican Party came along. When, occasionally, someone manages to win election to Congress under a third-party label or as an independent, they generally decide to caucus with one of the two major parties in exchange for committee assignments or other borrowed influence.

More Amazing

The durability and rigidity of Republicratism is even more amazing when you think about the changes over that period, including many instances in which the parties have traded positions on issues. It's almost impossible to draw a coherent line connecting the Republicans of Lincoln (a party entirely of the North, the pro-civil rights party that advocated for a muscular, activist federal government) and the Republicans of today. It's even more difficult when one notes that the Republican line had to pass through the trust-busting Teddy Roosevelt Era, the tragedy of the Hoover years and the moderation of the Eisenhower period.

But why? Why so durable and rigid a domination by the same two parties? I asked University of Minnesota political scientist and Congress expert Kathryn Pearson and she surprised me with a two-word reply that clearly seemed to answer the question (as long as you knew what the two words meant, which I did not). And the two words were: Duverger's Law.

Yes, Duverger's Law. Good ol' Maurice Duverger, possibly the most influential French political scientist of the 20th century, noted that the surest way to get a two-party system within a nation was to adopt "first-past-the-post" plurality voting with single-member districts. Translated, it refers to the system used in the vast majority of US elections, most specifically congressional elections. Every election for the US House (and most elections for city council members and county boards) are conducted according to the SMDP (single-member districts, plurality) voting system.

This forces those who might favor a minor party candidate to either vote for whichever of the two biggest parties the voter dislikes the least, or to risk the likelihood that their vote will be "wasted" or, worse, that they will end up helping the major-party candidate whom the voter dislikes the most to win. Minor parties aren't banned, but they seldom produce a plurality winner, and their lack of success often causes the minor parties to wither and die.

Third Parties Have to Win Elections to Gain Any Power

Steven Teles and Robert Saldin

Steven Teles is professor of political science at Johns Hopkins University. He is the author or co-author of several books, including The Captured Economy. *Robert Saldin is professor of political science at the University of Montana. He is the author of* When Bad Policy Makes Good Politics *and* War, the American State and Politics Since 1898.

Moderates have found the politics of the last few decades deeply depressing. While they once had considerable leverage in both major parties, they are now more likely to be scornfully dismissed if they're acknowledged at all. Yet the current political moment may offer moderates a rare opportunity to regain key footholds in the American political system. Doing so, however, will require them to shift their efforts away from doomed crusades like forging a new centrist party and toward the trench warfare of working within the existing two-party system. Chasing nonpartisan or anti-partisan fantasies may provide psychological comfort, but it's not going to generate much in the way of tangible results. Given the deep, self-reinforcing dynamics behind the disproportionate political influence of those at the ideological poles, no reform effort faces very attractive odds. That said, building moderate factions within the two major parties is the best investment of time, energy, and money for those who want a more deliberative, entrepreneurial, and productive political system.

The Moderates' Misunderstandings

American political parties have increasingly been captured by their ideological extremes and, as a consequence, the space for cross-party coalition-building has shrunk. Because our political institutions make it difficult to pass major policy reforms without support from both parties, the absence of moderates to bridge the divide means that polarization has generated legislative gridlock. Where moderates were once critical to building coalitions across party lines, both parties' leaders have established a hammerlock over the agenda in Congress, allowing only single-party coalitions to form except under very unusual conditions.[1] This process has been abetted by negative partisanship—that is, party attachment driven by fear and loathing of the other side more than a positive attachment to one's own party program—which has created a climate in which building bipartisan coalitions is seen as the equivalent of trading with the enemy.[2]

These familiar patterns have led ideological moderates to search for the bug in American institutions that is responsible for such extreme systemic dysfunction. Some have identified party primaries as the culprit and have embraced reforms like California's jungle primary or, more recently, ranked-choice voting.[3] Others blame the ideologically imbalanced structure of legislative districts and called for nonpartisan redistricting or judicial supervision of the redistricting process. Yet whatever desirable effects such reforms may bring, they have not produced a much higher number of moderate legislators, and thus our optimism about their potential to do so in the future should be limited.[4]

The failure of these kinds of reform mechanisms to spark a rebirth of moderation has led some moderates to conclude that the real problem lies with the Democratic and Republican parties themselves. Calling for a pox on both of their houses, these disenchanted moderates have fallen under the sway of one of the great chimeras of American politics: the exciting but ultimately Pollyannaish hope of creating a centrist third party to take on the two-party oligopoly. If we lived in a different country, a third party might be well worth exploring. But because the two-party system is baked into the cake of the American political system, the pursuit of a third party is guaranteed to be a sinkhole for money and energy.

Yet there is a more fundamental mistake behind all of these ideas for reform. They presume that the way to get more moderate legislators—and hence more moderate governance—is to change the rules of the game. To be sure, there is clearly something to the idea that the design of American institutions may be exacerbating political polarization and that changing them would make it easier for moderates to compete.[5] But the cold, hard truth is that moderates face a difficult, if not intractable, problem that institutional reforms will never be able to fully remedy. Even under optimal institutional rules, political outcomes are not determined by the mystical, disembodied median voter so much as they are by the blood, sweat, and tears of committed partisan actors. In the American political system, there are no shortcuts around the hard work of organization, mobilization, and engagement in the sometimes unseemly business of party politics.[6] To put it more bluntly, moderates lose to those on the ideological extremes because their adversaries—to their credit—actually do the hard, long-term work that democratic politics rewards.

Moderates, by contrast, have largely abandoned the field.[7] The wingnuts we so often deplore are often the ones who actually show up, organize, and devote themselves to building durable institutions for political and intellectual combat. Moderates, perhaps because they believe that the broad public is already with them, tend to believe that the control of politics by those mobilized at the ideological poles is illegitimate, and they look for ways to design rules to allow the sensible but unmobilized middle to have its preferences govern without having to do the hard work of organizing for action within the two major parties.

This is backwards. There is simply no way to get around the fact that democratic politics rewards participation and preference intensity, both at the mass and elite levels.[8] Energized actors at the poles have abundant incentives and resources to mobilize their supporters, and they have used that power to seize control of institutions—including the Republican and Democratic parties. Moderates have to wake up and realize that they need to do the same. Unless moderates increase their own commitment to durable, organized political activity, there is no institutional tweak that will keep them from losing out to those on the extremes.

Exploiting Fissures Within the Parties

In the past, moderates have relied on three alternatives to durable partisan organization. First, they have relied on the financial resources of moderate donors to pull the parties to the center, a strategy that has long since been ineffective with Republicans and which is increasingly running out of steam with Democrats (as we can see by the stigma on high-dollar fundraisers in the presidential primary and the increasing reliance on—and pious rhetoric attached to—small donations). Second, they have counted on their control of relatively insulated parts of government, such as the Federal Reserve and the foreign policy establishment. However, the power of both parties' moderate professionals—acutely in the Republican Party, and incrementally among the Democrats— appears to be diminishing, and strategies for further insulating various domains of government from partisan influence seem extremely unlikely in our populist age.[9] Third, moderates have taken advantage of the power of incumbency, drawing strength from members first elected in a less polarized era. But with each election cycle, these moderate incumbents are gradually replaced by new, more extreme members. Especially on the Republican side, the absence of collective organization means that moderates lack an ability to draw on a recognized, national brand that's distinct from their party's dominant, more extreme brand. As a result, they have to either quit—as most moderates have—or join the herd.

Their declining influence has led moderates to search for institutional reforms to amplify the voice of moderate voters. The most desperate indulge the Hail Mary scheme of forming a new, moderate third party. But while this search has paid the salary of many an otherwise unemployed political consultant, the dream of a moderate third party is futile, and not just because of the inescapability of Duverger's law in the American context (which is that a third party in a first-past-the-post system will inevitably hurt the major party it is closest to—that is, that it will backfire).[10] While there are many voters who don't fit naturally with the ideologies of the two parties, the largest such group is socially conservative and fiscally liberal.[11] That is the opposite of the Bloomberg/Schultz consensus of woke austerity that is the typical animating outlook for those pining for a third party.

The cruel truth is that there is no politically viable future for moderates outside the Democratic and Republican parties. And within those parties, moderates will only get the power that they desire by organizing as a coherent bloc, recruiting attractive candidates, mobilizing moderate voters in each party to participate in partisan politics, and developing ideas to inspire their base and provide opportunities for policy change. Without strong, durable, organizationally-dense factions, individual moderates or even entire state parties will not be able to distinguish themselves from their national brand or fight for leverage in national politics.[12] In other words, what influence moderates will have in the coming years will only emerge as a result of organizing as coherent minority factions within the Democratic and Republican parties.

But how can they do that when the two parties have been captured so thoroughly by their activist poles? Could moderate factions in the Democratic and Republican parties actually have any significant influence?

We think that they could and that moderates will have new opportunities to carve out footholds within the party system and thereby shape the country's future. The opening will come from deep forces at work in American society and politics that are going to cause the two parties to become less and less cohesive in the coming years. On the Republican side, Trumpist populism is making the party increasingly uncompetitive in the suburbs, creating political demand from some office-seekers for collective action that would allow them to distance themselves from the GOP's toxic national brand. Among Democrats, the temptation for overreach that accompanies the increasing power of the left in a number of coastal states will open up opportunities for Republicans who can split off suburban, relatively moderate Democrats with the promise of political adult supervision for left-wing legislative majorities. These forces have already created significant fissures within both parties that show no signs of abating. As these fissures widen, they will create an opportunity for organized and mobilized factions with different social and geographic bases to reemerge as a major force in American politics.

Under a scenario in which factions return, the control of Congress by party leadership will break down, as members will no longer consent to restrictive rules. When this occurs, the legislative agenda will become more chaotic and the opportunity for legislative entrepreneurship will expand. Habits of cross-party coalition-building that have faded in recent years will be rediscovered and the utility of constructing coalitions of strange bedfellows will increase. It's important to recognize that moderate factions don't need to be dominant to force such changes. Indeed, a relatively small—but pivotal—amount of disciplined moderate dissent in each party would be enough to provide the political leverage to demand rules changes conducive to greater cross-party agenda-setting. If that happened—and if supportive institutions, like think tanks, started supplying policy ideas with appeal across party lines—it would produce a Congress that has more in common with the early 1970s than the last quarter century.

If we are right, moderates—especially those with resources to devote to politics—should redirect their efforts. While the stage is set for factionalization in both parties, exploiting that opportunity will require the creation of durable institutions within each party designed to fight the battle for intraparty supremacy. Especially in the GOP, that is a battle that moderates cannot win in the sense of attaining dominance (at least in the foreseeable future). But, again, they do not need to attain primacy in the party in order to achieve many of their goals—they just need to pick, and win, the right battles.

The opportunity to gain sufficient power to change the operation of legislative institutions is emerging. But, crucially, that power will not simply be dropped in moderates' laps. This opportunity can be missed if moderate reformers devote their time to pointless democracy-reform do-goodism or quixotic third-partyism that does not build up a base of power in the two parties.

Ultimately, there is no nonpartisan route to the kind of looser, more deliberative democracy that many moderate reformers want. In the American political system, the only pathway is through the political parties. That may be uncomfortable for moderate donors in particular, who find partisan politics and the long, slow slog of political mobilization distasteful and prefer "practical problem solving" and yearn for government by experts. But ultimately, the path to improved democratic governance requires seizing power. If moderate votes, organizational activism, money, and ideas are not mobilized in the right places and over the long term, we will likely remain mired in hyperpolarized gridlock.

Distinct Factional Brands

Our current state of affairs makes it easy to forget that today's homogenous American parties are an anomaly, not the norm. More typically, the two major parties have each been deeply divided. This is an outgrowth of how our party system is structured. More specifically, two key ground rules in our electoral system overwhelmingly tilt the playing field toward a two-party system rather than a multiparty system. First, we have single-member districts in which each congressional and legislative district elects its own representative. Second, we have a winner-take-all system. This means that—unlike in a proportional system—garnering, say, 10 percent of the vote doesn't translate into 10 percent of the seats in legislative bodies. For third parties to gain any power, they have to actually win elections. This high standard for entry means that the two parties have an effective duopoly.

Because our institutions push strongly in the direction of two parties, it is no surprise that there has been no durable third party in the United States since the Republicans dislodged the Whigs in the 1850s. However, our enormous population, vast geography and demographic heterogeneity make it hard for those parties—especially in Congress—to be internally coherent. The consequence is that the ideological and coalitional diversity that other systems process through multiple parties has typically been institutionalized in the United States through durable factions within the two dominant political parties.[13]

Despite that, for the last couple decades both parties have been remarkably lacking in factional divisions. The Republicans in particular have not had organized groups with significantly different ideas, institutions, funders, and geographic bases. There has been, of course, the Freedom Caucus in the House of Representatives, but even there it disagreed with the leadership not on first principles but primarily on tactics.[14]

This era of internal coherence may be coming to an end. The Democrats are already seeing the first signs of durable factional divisions emerging in their ranks, with some members openly calling themselves socialists and rallying behind a presidential candidate— Bernie Sanders—who has always resisted membership in the party itself. This leftist wing of the party now has an increasingly large membership organization, the Democratic Socialists of America, that funnels party participation through a factional structure. The Democrats' left-wing has its own information networks, focused on social media. Increasingly, it also has its own think tanks—such as the Roosevelt Institute, Demos, New Consensus and Data for Progress—and magazines like *N+1* and *Jacobin* to provide their faction with ideas, such as the Green New Deal and Medicare For All. They also have their own ways to raise money, focused on large groups of small-dollar donors. Some members of this budding left faction of the Democrats, such as Justice Democrats, appear eager to openly challenge the party's leadership and will likely become even more aggressive as their ranks in the congressional caucus increase.

By contrast, the moderate wing of the party is somewhat less developed, although it has a significant base of large donors, a group of loosely affiliated members of Congress (the New Democrat Coalition) and a few think tanks like Third Way and the Progressive Policy Institute. But both of these factions are likely to only grow and deepen in the future, potentially squeezing politicians, activists, donors, campaign professionals, and intellectuals to join one faction or the other. It remains to be seen which faction will be dominant. The energy is certainly with the Democratic left for now, but it could be countered by growth in the moderate faction driven by refugees from an increasingly populist Republican Party. Whichever faction gains the upper hand, the Democrats in the future will almost certainly be a more deeply divided party than they have been since the fall of the conservative Southern Democrats.

The Republicans are likely to also become more factionally divided. Going forward, the dominant faction of the GOP will almost certainly be populist and nationalist, yet they will not have the party all to themselves. The populists are going to be forced to share the GOP with what we will call a liberal-conservative faction in recognition of their grounding in classical liberal principles of free trade, pluralism, and constitutionalism. The Republican Party in most of the South and Mountain West, along with a good part of the Midwest, will be Trumpist in character. But that dominant faction will be all but uncompetitive in the Southwest, the Pacific Coast, New England, and the Acela Corridor, even as far down as Virginia. Notably, these are the same parts of the country where the left wing of the Democrats will be the strongest, possibly even dominant. That leftist tilt will make the Democrats potentially beatable, especially in nonfederal races, by a Republican Party that embraces an individualist vision of racial and ethnic diversity; stands for economic competition and entrepreneurship; offers market mechanisms to protect the environment; promotes internationalism in foreign policy; and proposes aggressive measures to fight poverty and enhance economic mobility without growing the public payroll or handing over power to public-sector unions.

The core voters for this liberal-conservative faction will be the educated middle class, business, and more upwardly mobile parts of ethnic minority groups, especially in cities and states where Democratic governance starts to pinch their core interests. The faction will find significant financial support in the technology and finance sectors of the East and West Coasts (support it will share with moderate Democrats), which combine cultural liberalism with a pro-capitalist economics, albeit with a reformist bent. This faction will still be recognizably conservative, especially on secular questions of social order like crime and homelessness, opposition to public sector unions, and a general pro-market orientation.

The appeal and competitiveness of a Republican Party like that in the bluer parts of the country can already be seen in the reelection of Republican governors in Maryland and Massachusetts who, in a somewhat inchoate form, already embrace such an approach. Currently, these examples of GOP success in Annapolis and Beacon Hill are of the lone wolf variety. Fueling a durable faction with something more than charisma will require these leaders and their supporters to build a broader organization and forge connections with like-minded partisans elsewhere. Clearly Larry Hogan and Charlie Baker have not achieved anything of the sort. However, their success nonetheless offers some hope that building a liberal-conservative faction in the Republican Party is not a fantasy.

To be sure, this will be a minority faction. It will not be dominant in enough states to ever—with rare exceptions—form a majority in the Republicans' congressional party or get one of its adherents the GOP presidential nomination. But if it is able to develop a genuinely distinctive, independent factional brand—such that voters do not think of themselves as supporting the dominant, populist faction with their vote in congressional elections—it could be powerful enough that the majority faction is forced to negotiate and share power with it.

However, the nationalizing trends in American politics will make the creation of a distinct party factional brand challenging in ways that it has not been in the past. Americans are already becoming accustomed to voting in state and local elections on the basis of their national party preferences, for instance.[15] Nonetheless, the liberal-conservative wing of the Republican Party in particular will have some very impressive advantages with which to build a distinct brand. The nationalization of the media, for instance, will play into the hands of the liberal-conservatives since their strongholds are in the country's media centers. And because this faction will be particularly attractive to business interests in technology and finance,[16] it will have more than adequate resources to build institutions, fund candidates, and engage in intrapartisan warfare for control of state parties. It also will be especially attractive to the kinds of experts and thinkers who played such a key role in the Never Trump phenomenon and therefore will not lack for policies or well-developed public philosophies. Taken together, these are impressive resources with which to engage in faction-building.

The establishment of durable, organized factions along these lines would be a boon for moderates. Congress will look far different than the leadership-dominated institution to which we have become accustomed. In a world with more heterogeneous parties, neither party's majority leadership will be able to organize either chamber of Congress without reaching a bargain with its minority faction.[17] In exchange for their support in organizing Congress, the minority factions will insist upon institutional rules that significantly weaken the majority party leadership's exclusive control of the legislative agenda. This will be especially important because, in particular on issues of national security, trade, and immigration, the Republicans' liberal-conservative faction will have more in common with the Democrats' moderate faction than with its own party majority, and it will want the opportunity to legislate with its counterpart across the aisle. While frustrated with the minority moderate factions in their parties, the majority factions will have no choice but to work with them, since they will be competitive in places the majority factions are not. If the liberal-conservatives are able to develop a sufficiently distinct brand that can avoid the toxicity of the populist-nationalist Republican majority faction, they will be able to elect enough members of Congress to make the difference between a GOP majority and suffering in the minority. So while they will differ dramatically on policy, the GOP's factions will have a strong common interest in attaining institutional control. A similar dynamic will play out among the Democrats.

Fighting for Moderation

This return to factional political parties with the potential to reinvigorate the place of moderates in the American political system is a scenario, not a certainty. And it won't unfold purely on the basis of mechanical, structural forces. It is contingent on the existence of creative, intelligent agency on the part of individuals and organizations. A faction is composed of a network of organizations, and organizations do not emerge spontaneously. Moreover, there is no guarantee that they will be well-designed, well-led, sufficiently cunning, or endowed with enough resources flowing with the right incentives. In particular, the opportunity to build more factional parties depends upon the emergence of a core group of activists and donors who will provide the leadership and resources to build the structures through which a mobilized faction could emerge. Indeed, there is a significant danger than the very spirit that characterizes moderates—a tendency to eschew party politics—will lead their organization-building and reformist efforts into third-party or nonpartisan blind alleys.

Yet some of the raw materials of moderate factions in both parties already exist. Billionaire donors like Kathryn Murdoch and Seth Klarman are already starting to target their giving on building up political infrastructure for the parts of the parties that are neither populist nor socialist. But for these resources to have an impact, donors in both parties will need to shift their political activity toward consciously seeding the wide range of electoral, policy, and intellectual organizations that will allow moderates to gain leverage within institutions largely dominated by extremists. To take just one example, new magazines will need to form to provide ideas for the liberal-conservative faction of the Republican Party and the moderate faction of the Democrats, providing an outlet for affiliated academics, writers, and think tanks.

With the institutions of the national party largely out of their reach, activists, donors, and intellectuals alienated by the polarized direction of their respective party will need to redirect their activity into capturing and then building it up in places where it has desiccated. Where their parties are weak, moderates will have an opportunity to establish a power base for intraparty conflict. They will need to form new organizations of elected officials, along the lines of what the Democratic Leadership Council established in the 1980s, to create a political identity for aspiring officeholders distinct from the national party. If they are successful, they will translate their custody of state government, at least on occasion, into electing factional supporters to Congress and use their new institutions to coordinate their legislative efforts. The dominant populist faction of the Republican Party and the left faction of the Democratic Party may not even resist the growth of their minority factions, since they will operate in places where each party is nearly extinct, and success in those places may be necessary for controlling Congress in the future.

There is no question that on the Republican side, moderates are at a disadvantage in capturing state parties—even in places where the Trump brand is toxic—given that the president has such a dominant position among the party base. But that does not necessarily mean that the effort to build a power structure for Republicans in enough states to have influence is hopeless. Republican governors in blue states have especially powerful sway over their state parties and can use that to build a strong factional—as opposed to merely personal—base for moderation. In Virginia, for instance, the Trump brand has almost single-handedly destroyed the Republican Party's power in the state, making it uncompetitive in the middle-class suburbs that pave the way to control in Richmond. That suggests there could be demand from office-seekers for a rebranded party capable of differentiating itself from the increasingly toxic national brand by associating itself with a moderate faction. In Kansas, moderate Republicans openly defected from their more extreme conservative counterparts to reverse the sweeping tax cuts that wrecked the state's finances. More could and should be done to build that group into a durable faction in the state legislature. Even more broadly, moderate Republicans in a few states such as these need to focus on actually organizing ordinary citizens who agree with them—which in some places will include Democrats defecting from a party that is increasingly controlled by the left—to compete for control of their state parties. That will be the work of more than a year or two, but it is the kind of long-term effort that has given conservatives the whip hand in the party.

Conclusion

The scenario we sketch above is certainly not the only possibility, but it is internally consistent and makes sense of various pieces of activity and networks that are already in place. It also suggests that by developing factions within each party, moderates have a golden opportunity to reemerge as a power center in American politics. While they may seem like unicorns in our current, polarized moment, factions used to be the norm in American politics and the time is ripe for their reemergence. But it's not going to happen on its own. Moderates will have to summon the motivation and discipline that already drive their competitors.

Endnotes

1. Lawrence Evans, *The Whips* (Ann Arbor: University of Michigan Press, 2018).

2. Lilliana Mason, *Uncivil Agreement: How Politics Became Our Identity* (Chicago: University of Chicago Press, 2018); Douglas J. Ahler and Gaurav Sood, "The Parties in Our Heads: Misperceptions About Party Composition and Their Consequences," *Journal of Politics* 80:3 (2018), 964-981.

3. Frances McCall Rosenbluth and Ian Shapiro, *Responsible Parties* (New Haven: Yale University Press, 2018).

4. Simon Waxman, "Ranked-Choice Voting Is Not the Solution," *Democracy Journal*, 3 Nov. 2016; Taylor Larson and Joshua A. Duden, "Vying to Be King of the Jungle: Where Top-Two Primaries Fall Short," *Concordia Law Review* 4:1 (2019).

5. Lee Drutman, *Breaking the Two-Party Doom Loop* (New York: Oxford University Press, 2020); Greg Koger and Matthew Lebo, *Strategic Party Government* (Chicago: University of Chicago Press, 2017); Frances Lee, *Insecure Majorities* (Chicago: University of Chicago Press, 2016).

6. Ruth Bloch Rubin, *Building the Bloc: Intraparty Organization in the US Congress* (New York: Cambridge University Press, 2017).

7. See, for instance, Danielle M. Thomsen, *Opting Out of Congress: Partisan Polarization and the Decline of Moderate Candidates* (New York: Cambridge University Press, 2018).

8. Benjamin Bishin, *Tyranny of the Minority* (Philadelphia: Temple University Press, 2009).

9. Jonathan Rauch and Raymond J. La Raja, "Re-Engineering Politicians: How Activist Groups Choose Our Candidates—Long Before We Vote," Brookings Institution Report, 7 Dec. 2017; Thomsen, *Opting Out*.

10. Patrick Dunleavy observes that Duverger's law seems to apply only in the United States. But there it applies ruthlessly. https://blogs.lse.ac.uk/politicsandpolicy/duvergers-law-dead-parrot-dunleavy/.

11. Lee Drutman, "Opposing Forces," Democracy Fund Voter Study Group, Aug. 2019; Morris P. Fiorina, *Disconnect: The Breakdown of Representation in American Politics* (Norman: University of Oklahoma Press, 2011).

12. Bloch Rubin, *Building the Bloc*; Daniel DiSalvo, *Engines of Change: Party Factions in American Politics, 1868-2010* (New York: Oxford University Press, 2010).

13. On the role of factions in American political parties across history, see DiSalvo, *Engines of Change*.

14. Rachel M. Blum, *How the Tea Party Captured the GOP* (Chicago: University of Chicago Press, 2019); Matthew Green, *Legislative Hardball: The House Freedom Caucus and the Power of Threat-Making in Congress* (New York: Cambridge University Press, 2019).

15. Dan Hopkins, *The Increasingly United States: How and Why American Political Behavior Nationalized* (Chicago: University of Chicago Press, 2018).

16. Evidence that technology entrepreneurs in particular are not an ideal fit for either party—but would be a very good fit for a liberal-conservative faction of the Republicans—can be found in David Broockman, Gregory Ferenstein, and Neil Malhotra, "Predispositions and the Political Behavior of American Economic

Elites: Evidence from Technology Entrepreneurs," *American Journal of Political Science* (Jan. 2019), 212-233.

17. This argument draws on "conditional party government" theory, the most important examples of which are David W. Rohde, *Parties and Leaders in the Postreform House* (Chicago: University of Chicago Press, 1991) and John Aldrich, *Why Parties? The Origin and Transformation of Political Parties in America* (Chicago: University of Chicago Press, 1995).

Organizations to Contact

The editors have compiled the following list of organizations concerned with the issues debated in this book. The descriptions are derived from materials provided by the organizations. All have publications or information available for interested readers. This list was compiled on the date of publication of the present volume; the information provided here may change. Be aware that many organizations take several weeks or longer to respond to inquiries, so allow as much time as possible.

American Civil Liberties Union (ACLU)
125 Broad Street, 18th Floor
New York, NY 10004
(212) 549-2500
website: www.aclu.org

The American Civil Liberties Union (ACLU) is a nonprofit organization that was founded in 1920 with the intention of defending the individual rights and liberties guaranteed by the Constitution, including the right to vote. It has filed numerous lawsuits across the US to help secure and protect voting rights. It also launched the Let People Vote campaign to inform the public on their voting rights, provide them information on how to vote by mail, and keep them updated on important election deadlines.

Center for American Progress
1333 H Street NW, 10th Floor
Washington, DC 20005
(202) 682-1611
website: www.americanprogress.org

The Center for American Progress is a progressive-leaning nonprofit public policy research and advocacy organization. It was founded in 2003 with the intention of promoting an effective government with progressive ideals that benefit all Americans by helping shape political policy and inform voters. It publishes detailed reports on election security across the fifty states and America's electoral future, among other issues.

Constitution Party

PO Box 1782
Lancaster, PA 17608
(800) 283-8647
email: contactcp@constitutionparty.com
website: www.constitutionparty.com

The Constitution Party is a conservative American political third party that was founded in 1990 and known as the US Taxpayers' Party until 1999. Its mission is to uphold an originalist interpretation of the principles of the US Constitution. It focuses on limiting the power of the federal government to the enumerated functions listed in the Constitution and eliminating taxation whenever possible.

Democracy in Action

PO Box 19007
Washington, DC 20036
(310) 496-9633
email: action08@gmail.com
website: www.democracyinaction.us

Democracy in Action is an independent news website that was launched in 1998 to help readers follow and understand presidential campaigns. It looks at presidential candidates, including major third party candidates, to help readers understand their platform, campaign team, political and personal background, and party affiliation. It also provides other information on factors that impact elections, such as interest groups and campaign communications.

Democratic Socialists of America (DSA)
PO Box 1038
New York, NY 10272
email: yds@dsausa.org
website: www.dsausa.org

The Democratic Socialists of America (DSA) is the largest socialist organization in the United States. It focuses on building progressive movements for social change by promoting gender and racial equality, protecting the environment, and ending brutality and violence in defense of the status quo. It includes a youth section made up of college and high school students called Young Democratic Socialists of America (YDSA). Its website includes information on current DSA candidates and initiatives and details on how to get involved.

Election Law at Moritz
The Ohio State University
Michael E. Moritz College of Law
55 West 12th Avenue
Columbus, OH 43210
(614) 292-2631
email: thomson.165@osu.edu

The Election Law program at the Moritz College of Law of the Ohio State University is a nonpartisan research, education, and outreach program. It brings together the public, lawyers, academics, educators, journalists, policymakers, civic leaders, and election administrators to better understand issues related to the world of election administration. It was founded in 2004, and its longest-running and most notable project is the Major Pending Election Cases project, which provides case summaries, court filings, and expert commentary about notable election law cases from around the country in an accessible manner.

Green Party of the United States (GPUS)
PO Box 75075
Washington, DC 20013
(202) 319-7191
email: office@gp.org
website: www.gp.org

The Green Party of the United States (GPUS) is an independent political third party that is connected to American social movements and the global green movement. Its four pillars are peace and nonviolence, ecological wisdom, grassroots democracy, and social justice. It has more than 100 elected officials around the country, mostly at the municipal level, and it does not accept corporate donations.

HeadCount
104 West 29th Street, 11th Floor
New York, NY 10001
(866) 687-8683
email: info@headcount.org
website: www.headcount.org

HeadCount is a nonpartisan nonprofit organization that works with musicians to encourage participation in democracy in the US. It does this by registering voters at concerts and on the internet, informing voters on political issues, and encouraging participation in the census. The organization has registered over 600,000 voters since 2004 and worked with numerous musicians, including Ariana Grande, Beyoncé, members of the Grateful Dead, and Jay-Z.

Libertarian Party
Libertarian National Committee, Inc.
1444 Duke Street
Alexandria, VA 22314
(800) 353-2887
email: info@lp.org
website: www.lp.org

The Libertarian Party is an American political third party that focuses on promoting individual freedoms, limiting government interference in personal and business decisions, and reducing taxation. It was founded in 1971 and runs hundreds of candidates every election cycle, from local to national. Its website provides information on the party's political platform, details about current Libertarian candidates, and news related to Libertarian Party initiatives.

Rock the Vote
1440 G Street NW
Washington, DC 20005
(202) 719-9910
email: info@rockthevote.org
website: www.rockthevote.org

Rock the Vote is a nonprofit progressive-aligned organization. It was founded in 1990 by music industry executives to encourage young people to vote. It uses popular media, technology, and culture to empower new voters and give them the information they need to vote. Its website includes information on registering to vote and becoming a poll worker for elections.

Bibliography

Books

Omar H. Ali. *In the Balance of Power: Independent Black Politics and Third-Party Movements in the United States.* Athens, OH: Ohio University Press, 2020.

Michael Barone. *How America's Political Parties Change (and How They Don't).* New York, NY: Encounter Books, 2019.

David Boaz. *The Libertarian Mind: A Manifesto for Freedom.* New York, NY: Simon & Schuster, 2015.

Richard Davis, ed. *Beyond Donkeys and Elephants: Minor Political Parties in Contemporary American Politics.* Lawrence, KS: University Press of Kansas, 2020.

Lee Drutman. *Breaking the Two-Party Doom Loop: The Case for Multiparty Democracy in America.* New York, NY: Oxford University Press, 2020.

Katherine M. Gehl and Michael E. Porter. *The Politics Industry: How Political Innovation Can Break Partisan Gridlock and Save Our Democracy.* Boston, MA: Harvard Business Review Press, 2020.

Daniel Klinghard. *The Nationalization of American Political Parties, 1880–1896.* New York, NY: Cambridge University Press, 2014.

Barbara Krasner, ed. *The Two-Party System in the United States* (Current Controversies). New York, NY: Greenhaven Publishing, 2019.

L. Sandy Maisel. *American Political Parties and Elections: A Very Short Introduction.* New York, NY: Oxford University Press, 2016.

Richard A. McFarlane. *The Only-Two-Party System: Why Third Parties Are Unconstitutional.* Orange, CA: Lex Scripta Legal Research Group, 2014.

Ralph Nader. *Breaking Through Power: It's Easier Than We Think.* San Francisco, CA: City Lights Books, 2016.

Alex Prichard, Ruth Kinna, Saku Pinta, and David Berry, eds. *Libertarian Socialism: Politics in Black and Red.* Oakland, CA: PM Press, 2017.

Charles Prysby. *Rich Voter, Poor Voter, Red Voter, Blue Voter: Social Class and Voting Behavior in Contemporary America.* New York, NY: Routledge, 2020.

Kathleen Sears. *Socialism 101: From the Bolsheviks and Karl Marx to Universal Healthcare and the Democratic Socialists: Everything You Need to Know About Socialism.* Holbrook, MA: Adams Media, 2019.

Bhaskar Sunkara. *The Socialist Manifesto: The Case for Radical Politics in an Era of Extreme Inequality.* New York, NY: Basic Books, 2020.

Periodicals and Internet Sources

Alex Ashlock and Jeremy Hobson, "How Ross Perot's Third Party Presidential Bids Shook Up American Politics," NPR, July 10, 2019. https://www.wbur.org/hereandnow /2019/07/10/perot-third-party-presidential-bids.

Bente Birkeland, "With Voters Sour on Major Parties, Group Recruits 'None of the Above' Candidates," NPR, October 14, 2018. https://www.npr.org/2018/10/14/656576055/with -voters-sour-on-major-parties-group-recruits-none-of-the -above-candidates.

David Brooks, "Opinion: The Third-Party Option," *New York Times,* July 30, 2018. https://www.nytimes.com/2018/07/30 /opinion/third-party-2020-election-localism.html.

Gail Collins, "Opinion: Presidentially, Two Parties Is Plenty," *New York Times*, September 16, 2020. https://www.nytimes.com/2020/09/16/opinion/third-parties-2020.html.

Michael Brendan Dougherty, "We Need More Libertarianism Too," *National Review*, April 7, 2020. https://www.nationalreview.com/2020/04/coronavirus-response-we-need-more-libertarianism/.

David Duhalde, "This Vermont Gubernatorial Nominee Is Showing How Successful Third Parties Are Possible," *Jacobin*, September 15, 2020. https://www.jacobinmag.com/2020/09/vermont-governor-progressive-party-bernie-sanders.

Juleanna Glover, "Opinion: Are Republicans Ready to Join a Third Party?" *New York Times*, January 29, 2018. https://www.nytimes.com/2018/01/29/opinion/republicans-third-party-.html.

Durin Hendricks, "Minor Parties in US Make Gains in Local Elections," *VOA News*, November 12, 2019. https://www.voanews.com/usa/us-politics/minor-parties-us-make-gains-local-elections.

Pedro Hernandez, "The United States' History of Third Party Candidates: Is the Problem with Third Parties or with Our Binary Election System?" FairVote, May 19, 2020. https://www.fairvote.org/the_united_states_history_of_third_party_candidates_is_the_problem_with_third_parties_or_with_our_binary_election_system.

Alexandra Jaffe, "By the Numbers: Third-Party Candidates Had an Outsize Impact on Election," *NBC News*, November 8, 2016. https://www.nbcnews.com/storyline/2016-election-day/third-party-candidates-having-outsize-impact-election-n680921.

Joshua Jamerson, "Third Parties See Diminished Support in 2020 Race," *Wall Street Journal*, September 16, 2020. https://

www.wsj.com/articles/third-parties-see-diminished -support-in-2020-race-11600254002.

Bill McKibben, "Instead of Challenging Joe Biden, Maybe the Green Party Should Help Change Our Democracy," *New Yorker*, April 15, 2020. https://www.newyorker.com/news /daily-comment/instead-of-challenging-joe-biden-maybe -the-green-party-could-help-change-our-democracy.

Peter Slevin, "The Many, Tangled American Definitions of Socialism," *New Yorker*, June 14, 2019. https://www .newyorker.com/news/dispatch/the-many-tangled -american-definitions-of-socialism.

Matt Welch, "Third Parties: Barred from the Debates, Impacting Polls Only Marginally," *Reason*, September 29, 2020. https:// reason.com/2020/09/29/third-parties-barred-from-the -debates-impacting-polls-only-marginally/.

Index